SCHOLASTIC

C000184368

YOU CAN

Be an Effective
SUBJECT
LEADER

Anthony David

FOR AGES
4-11

"Effective leadership is vital, if we are to achieve a world-class education system…"

Lord Andrew Adonis, 2007

Acknowledgements

Author
Anthony David

Editor
Nicola Morgan

Development Editor
Kate Pedlar

Project Editor
Fabia Lewis

Series Designer
Catherine Perera

Cover Designer
Anna Oliwa/Rebecca Male

Cover photography
© iofoto/www.stockxpert.com

Design
Q2A Media

Text © Anthony David
© 2009 Scholastic Ltd

Designed using Adobe InDesign

Published by Scholastic Ltd
Villiers House
Clarendon Avenue
Leamington Spa
Warwickshire CV32 5PR

www.scholastic.co.uk

Printed by Bell and Bain Ltd.
1 2 3 4 5 6 7 8 9 9 0 1 2 3 4 5 6 7 8

The author dedicates this book to David, Anthea, Robin and Lily Cox.

© Crown copyright and other materials reproduced under the terms of the Click Use Licence. Extracts from The Bichard Inquiry Report by Sir Michael Bichard © Parliamentary copyright 2004. National College of School Leadership for the use of extracts from *The Role and Purpose of Middle Leaders in School* © 2003, NCSL (2003, NCSL).
Wisconsin Department of Public Instruction for the use of 'Key Ideas' from *Characteristics of Successful Schools* (© 2008, Wisconsin Department of Public Instruction).

British Library Cataloguing-in-Publication Data
A catalogue record for this book is available from the British Library.
ISBN 978-1407-10195-8

Contents

Contents

Introduction

Within 12 to 24 months of teaching you will find yourself responsible for an aspect of school life (endearingly referred to as a 'hat' by many colleagues). The number of 'hats' you wear will depend on the size of the school and, although these areas of responsibility will vary in theme, how you approach them will be much the same. Your personal organisation, resource management and the systems you introduce are all part of the day-to-day management of your subject. However, in recent years the language of subject management has changed.
It wasn't that long ago when these responsibilities were considered aspects of school coordination. Thinking has moved on and, with it, so has the language of post-holders – you are now a leader. Middle leadership is the beating heart of the school: you are the flag bearer and champion of your subject, and it is your enthusiasm that drives your subject forward. Your guidance is what motivates subject improvement and it is your leadership that empowers colleagues to change.

Leading a subject from the classroom

Leading a subject from the classroom requires a new set of skills. As a teacher you are trained to teach. Picking up the necessary skill set for subject leadership requires discipline and a pragmatic approach to what you need to do versus what you are able to accomplish in the time you have. Fortunately, thinking on their feet is something that teachers are good at doing!

It is an exciting time to be a part of school leadership. Extended schools and children's centres are just two major influences on the school community. Indeed, the community itself now has greater access than before, through breakfast clubs and other forms of child care. Schools are also embracing core services, such as health and social services, to support their community and the families they serve within it. It is a period of great change and one that will, no doubt, impact on your subject leadership. It is a wonderful opportunity to embrace parents as co-educators of their children and to give them licence to take on this role.

This book focuses on how you can manage and lead your subject on a day-to-day basis and from a whole-school perspective. It aims to provide you with a range of tools and resources that you can use to support your leadership. Being the champion for a subject is exciting. With it you have the opportunity to direct and shape a whole aspect of school life, which can have a life-long impact on the children and families you support.

You Can... Define your roles and responsibilities

Taking on a leadership role within the school ultimately means that your job has new responsibilities. Many of these will be clearly set out within your leadership job description. At the core of this will be responsibility for subject action planning and managing your budget. This will form the backbone of what you are doing that year based on identified need from the previous year. That said, there are times when you may be required to support the school in areas not specified on your Teaching and Learning Responsibility (TLR) job description. This is when leadership gets creative!

Thinking points

● Communication is a fundamental part of your role. Historically this would have been centred on the school but now, with digital technologies such as texting and emailing, the communication range has grown. Consider how you communicate with families, consultants and other schools. Is your communication as effective as it could be?

● Increasingly schools are being driven by projects rather than subjects. A School Leadership Team should be aware that their TLR or leadership points reflect a degree of responsibility rather than a specific subject and those areas of responsibility should change according to the school's needs.

● It is challenging to motivate oneself at a high level all the time and it is not desirable. Plan your time carefully and allow for low-level tasks, such as filing, to balance your day. Be in control of your job and not the other way round.

Tips, ideas and activities

● Do you clearly understand your roles and responsibilities? If you are not sure then ask the headteacher for a copy of your job description and information about your TLR points.

● Be mindful that your role is likely to change as educational reforms impact on you, your school and your subject. Equally, when you take on more responsibility you will, in all likelihood, have to evaluate how you manage your leadership time in order to fulfil all your responsibilities.

● What professional development have you taken part in over the last year? Has this supported your practice?

● Part of your job will be to problem-solve, so be prepared to think outside the box and to accept ideas from other colleagues. Make staff aware of local opportunities that can support your subject and enhance the school's involvement with the local community.

● Work closely with your local authority or diocese as they will be your primary link to changes within education.

● Maintain a positive outlook. Yes, this is a challenging job but keeping a realistic and positive view will support morale. Be professional. Your professional beliefs, coupled with the school's aims, should support most of your decisions and actions.

● Your budget may well be set by the school and in most cases is a nominal sum. However, a robust action plan should be able to demonstrate where additional funding is required and can be used to support any argument for an enhanced budget.

You Can... Identify leadership characteristics

Leadership is, somewhat surprisingly, a new word within education. Pre-millennial teachers were managers and the only rightful leader was seen to be the headteacher. Yet all teachers display leadership characteristics from the moment they enter the classroom. There should be little surprise that where there is a strong teacher there is also a subject leader in waiting. The skills are essentially the same. While it is true that no two leaders are the same, what most leaders share is a passion for their vision, a defined understanding of their own strengths and a desire to grow the potential of those who surround them.

Thinking points

● Warren Bennis, an American scholar widely regarded as the pioneer in the field of leadership studies, differentiated managers from leaders by saying that 'Managers are people who do things right, while leaders are people who do the right thing.' (*Leaders: The Strategies for Taking Charge* by Bennis and Nanus, Harper and Row, 1985) The step up from a manager to a leader is achieved by people who look at what needs to be done and how to do it.

● Leadership styles are changing within schools. The old model of top-down, headteacher-style leadership is being flattened out to embrace a wider, distributed model of leadership. The advantages of this model are that they support middle and senior leaders with genuine powers of responsibility, while freeing the head from many day-to-day tasks to concentrate on leading the vision and ethos of the school.

Tips, ideas and activities

● Be honest – display integrity and sincerity in all your actions. Deceptive behaviour will not inspire trust and is easy to spot.

● Be competent – do what you say you are going to do. Delegate so that what you say can be done will be.

● Understand your vision – effective leaders envision what they want and how to get it. They consistently pick priorities based on their basic values.

● Inspire – display confidence in all that you do. Know how to teach and have a full appreciation of the educational world. Take charge when necessary but show flexibility in your leadership style.

● Be current – keep up to date with current practice and ideas. Attend briefings and read reports.

● Be tolerant – seek out diversity.

● Take risks – have the perseverance to accomplish a goal, regardless of obstacles. Look confident and calm under stress.

● Be a plain speaker – listen to your own sound judgement to make good decisions even when time is against you.

● Be available – it's not always possible to be around when people need you but setting aside times to run a clinic (always popular if you are the ICT leader) can help you to manage your time and give people a slot when they can talk to you.

● Be creative – things do not always go to plan but the creative leader will look for an opportunity where there appears to be none.

You Can... Identify your leadership style

Knowing your strengths and how you react in situations is vital to being a successful leader. Page 7 outlines desirable leadership attitudes; however knowing your style is what drives your leadership forward. Colleagues will know your core style, in some cases better than you, but understanding what other styles are present will help you to switch between them in different leadership situations. A good leader will not only use those characteristics that define their own particular style but will adopt other approaches when the need arises.

Thinking points

● There are many different styles of leadership. Search the internet for 'leadership styles' and you will be presented with styles including charismatic, micro-leaders, participative, situational, autocratic, democratic, seagull managers (those who swoop in, poop on your head and then swoop out again), transformational leaders and the list goes on. What you adopt as your own personal style will be dependent on your personal values, experiences and beliefs and will no doubt be a mix of many styles. This is normal, but having a consideration of other styles will allow you to adapt appropriately in different situations.

● When adopting a style, consider the influencing factors such as your relationships with others, your stress levels and who you are working with. You may need to adopt different styles for different situations, for example, to challenge the group you are working with or to speed up the process.

Tips, ideas and activities

● What sort of leader do you think you are? Are you a considered leader, or one who drives progress through his or her own enthusiasm or charisma? The US Army in 1973 identified three core types of leadership: autocratic, participative and the delegator. Although a classroom is a long way away from the 1970's American Army, the three styles are commonly found where there is leadership and should be considered.

● An autocrat is a person who tells their colleagues what they want, how they want it done and does not ask whether or not it can be done another way. This is an appropriate style if you are short of time or if you hold all the information but it should be used sparingly.

● The participative approach involves other colleagues in the decision-making process. This demonstrates that you value colleagues' input and that you do not have all the information in order to make a fair judgement. If you value your colleagues' skill and knowledge this will draw them into your team allowing you to make better decisions collectively.

● A delegator allows the group full delegation to work independently. This does not mean that you devolve any responsibility but is a recognition that they are good at what they are doing and do not need your hands-on support. It is important to be aware that this can be abused, allowing teams to move so far away from your core purpose that they are no longer working to the benefit of the whole team.

You Can... **Lead from the classroom**

There is a delicate juggling act between leading a classroom and leading a subject. Both roles demand time but how you lead your classroom will influence expectations about how you lead your subject area. A clearly organised classroom can be a good indicator to an organised approach to leading a subject (though not necessarily always true).

Thinking points

● How do you manage your furniture? There are various desk arrangements and each has advantages and disadvantages. Victorian-style rows are well-suited for paired work, which is how children naturally work. However, it feels traditional and is not particularly sociable. A horseshoe arrangement is useful for class discussions but requires a lot of space. Standard group tables (three tables, six chairs) save space and are sociable. However, children still tend to work in pairs and sometimes may want to work by themselves, which can be difficult on a group table. Adopting a flexible policy keeps the learning environment fresh, allowing children to experience different learning models.

● Carpet time and where you place your carpet needs careful consideration. Time spent on the carpet varies across the school years. It should be managed and be no longer than 20–30 minutes.

Tips, ideas and activities

● Delegate jobs to your children. This works well on a rolling programme because low-level tasks tend be done well when they are new. Tasks such as handing out books, tidying areas, group organisation and other responsibilities can support continuity in the classroom when you are away and asserts your authority on the class.

● Keep planning current. This does not mean reams and reams of planning, far from it; it should be succinct and driven by the needs of the children. If you keep it open on your desk as you take the lesson, you can make notes as you go along. This is common practice in the Foundation Stage where many teachers also use large sticky notes to add comments. This gives life to your planning and prevents it from being retrospective.

● Keep your assessments up to date, particularly identifying children with special needs, including very able children.

● While the class are tidying their desks, take time to tidy yours. A clutter-free teacher's desk is a positive example for children.

● Have a clear timetable. This does not mean that you cannot manoeuvre away from it (that's half the fun of teaching in primary schools) but it gives a clear indication of what you are planning to do and when during the week.

● Keep displays current, particularly any displays that are associated with your subject. Ensure they are well-mounted, clearly labelled, represent a wide range of abilities and children, and have a clear title.

● Children love to hear what you are learning about or what you are interested in. It may be a language, an art project, a book you are writing or learning to ice skate! Learning should be fun.

● Look at other colleagues' classrooms. You can always find at least one trick in another colleague's classroom that you can include in your own!

You Can... Identify your impact on children's learning

The experience that children are getting in schools is becoming broader and broader, which is no bad thing. However, your core purpose is enabling children to learn and with that you need to measure what impact your teaching is having on a child. Being able to measure your impact requires a range of strategies that are based on a fundamental baseline understanding of the children in your care. Knowing the children gives you a platform on which to base any learning measurements.

Thinking points

● Children learn best when they are reasonably challenged in a safe environment that celebrates success and enjoys achievement.

● The importance of the parents'/carers' role in preparing and supporting their child cannot be underestimated. For most parents, school was a positive experience when they were a child but there are some for whom it will have been an entirely different experience. A parent's negative school experience will, in all likelihood, have an impact on their child's learning. If a school is in a position to identify this early (and parents who had a negative experience at school are often willing to say so), then calming their fears by leading that parent through the rich, modern learning environment that is offered to their child is time well spent.

Tips, ideas and activities

A range of strategies can be used to assess the impact that teaching of your subject has on learning across the school. Below are some suggestions about how to collect this evidence:

● Go on a 'learning walk'. By spending time popping into classes you can gather a range of information including the subject's profile and possibly see a couple of lessons. This will give you a snap-shot of what is happening across the school.

● Speak to children. Interviewing a range of children will help you understand what they know about your subject. It also allows them to express their view and showcase their knowledge.

● Scrutinise books. A traditional book scrutiny can quickly show progression and can provide useful evidence when identifying academic trends across the school.

● Look at extended learning opportunities. Take into account opportunities for children such as after-school clubs, school visits and guest speakers.

● Talk to your colleagues. What impact do they feel they are having on the children in their class? A skills audit (see page 34) can highlight good practice in your school.

● Use summative assessment and tracking procedures. These are invaluable tools when assessing the core curriculum subjects. With these, core subject leaders should be able to closely monitor the impact of teaching on learning across the school and, where necessary, provide the relevant professional development.

You Can... Find opportunities to lead

As a middle leader, finding the opportunities to lead can be a challenge in itself. Demands on whole-school leadership are driven by school improvement priorities, the school Self-Evaluation Form (SEF) and the school vision. But, being a subject's champion gives you reasonable licence to keep its profile high, regardless of whether the subject is in focus that year or not. Looking for leadership opportunities keeps your subject's profile high and can be done through other channels aside from the School Leadership Team or whole staff, such as the school council or parent forums to support home learning.

Thinking points

● It is good practice for a school to have an aspect of one of the core subjects as a school improvement priority, however this doesn't leave much room for the foundation subjects. Schools are increasingly coming up with creative solutions to this with themed weeks or projects during the year to highlight other areas of the curriculum. Alternatively, your school may take a long-term view by focusing on two foundation subjects per year, effectively covering the foundation subjects in four years. This does not exclude on-going work but allows for planned, in-depth analysis.

● Increasingly, subject leaders are leading areas that fall outside of the curriculum. Areas such as Every Child Matters, international links and sustainability are all new and important themes that require leadership. There is no reason why these subjects should not be managed and led in the same way as traditional areas.

Tips, ideas and activities

● At heart you are the champion for your subject. Ensure you are well-informed so that you can give current advice.

● Enthusiasm for your subject is contagious. Often we are asked to be a 'jack of all trades' in primary schools but be realistic with the areas you are leading. It will be easier for you and you will be more effective if it is something that you are genuinely excited about.

● Consult with the School Leadership Team (SLT). You will most likely be required to write an action plan (which you should be preparing in July, allowing a full academic year for its delivery starting in September) from which you can identify areas that require significant support. You could ask to be invited to a meeting to allow you to present these to the SLT.

● Evening training sessions are quickly filled at the start of the year, mainly with seasonal training that happens year after year, such as assessment or NQT training. If you want to request a training session for your subject then it is useful to present that request to the SLT as soon as possible, ideally before the end of the prior term or academic year.

● You may wish to buddy up with two other subject leaders to present a series of workshops where, instead of the standard staffroom training, you set up a series of three workshops around the school and present 20 or 30 minute micro-training sessions. These are useful as they present a lot of information quickly and generate their own energy.

● Leading a subject on your own can be a challenge. A shadow leader or team structure that recruits other adults into your subject area, such as teaching assistants or parents, can support your leadership and spread your core message.

You Can... Wear more than one hat

Teachers are among the best qualified at multi-tasking. I recently observed a skilled reception teacher leading a phonics lesson as she directed another adult in her class to work with a small group, and then reached out to collect some books from the book corner to illustrate a point while wiping a child's nose. It was masterful, and something that teachers do day in, day out. Added to this are the complexities of leading a subject, which in small schools often means more than one subject. So, how can this be done without tying yourself in knots?

Thinking points

● The lion's share of your energy will, naturally, be given to your class. However, colleagues will, with good reason, expect sharp leadership if they ask you something about your subject area. Knowing this, consider how you pace your weeks, terms and year. See page 56 for a suggested model of events that can form the backbone of how you pace your work.

● It is easy to forget, but important to remember, that as the term progresses energy levels drop. As a leader you need to demonstrate that you are able to manage your workload which, particularly by the end of the academic year, may mean saying no. This should be done sensitively (after all, your colleague is as tired as you) and does not mean that you haven't logged the conversation for future reference.

Tips, ideas and activities

● Keep your diary with you. There is nothing worse than a colleague feeling as though they have reasonably asked you for something that you appear to have forgotten about. A diary or notebook means that at least if you are caught in the corridor, you can make a note of the request. Better still, arrange a time to talk to the colleague when you can give the discussion your considered time.

● Keep clear files for each subject area. Page 39 describes what a good file should contain and, if all your files have a similar approach to their contents, this will help you access information quickly.

● File paperwork when you receive it. This is the best way to keep on top of paperwork and the fastest way to lose control over your files if you don't!

● Be realistic with your focus. It may be that an aspect of one of your subjects is part of the School Improvement Plan (SIP) for that year. It is reasonable to expect that most of your energies will be given to that area. This does not mean that you ignore other leadership responsibilities, far from it, as they are your responsibility but it is reasonable to assume that this will be a focus.

● Use non-contact time wisely. PPA and leadership time (all part of the new arrangements for teachers) can be used as you see fit. Knowing that there is a natural cycle to school life, plan dates into your diary when you will be looking at your budget, observing lessons, writing your action plan, corresponding with governors. If events are planned for, then however many subjects you lead, your workload will not feel quite so daunting.

You Can... **Be a good speaker**

Public speaking is inevitable for subject leaders. Ultimately you will be required to share your vision and will need to do that in a way that a range of audiences can digest. In most cases these will be your colleagues but, increasingly, subject leaders are being invited to governors' meetings to give briefings or to present curriculum events to the whole school community.

Thinking points

● PowerPoint® presentations look smart but overly long slide presentations can also be dull. To avoid 'death by PowerPoint', keep your slides to a minimum. Do not be tempted by animations as they can distract from, rather than add to, a talk. People recall images more readily than lists, which you should keep in mind when planning your talk.

● Public speaking is an unnatural way of communicating. We are geared towards discussion, which involves knowing who we are talking to, interjecting, talking in slang and breaking sentences. Knowing that, public speakers must use tools to create the sense of a conversation. Rhetorical questions, laughter, using props and images are all useful tools that public speakers can lean on to break up their own voice.

Tips, ideas and activities

● Aim to keep your message clear and succinct, and refer to it regularly.

● Clearly set out what you are going to cover in the talk. Use headings as a reference when talking and then review them in your conclusion. As a man once said *tell them what you are going to talk about; talk about it; then tell them what you told them.*

● Avoid using jargon, explain acronyms (even if they are familiar), and keep your language simple. A simple message is easy to remember and hard to forget.

● Get your audience talking. If you talk for more than 10 minutes without a break, you will begin to lose your audience. If this is not possible then pose rhetorical questions, which will at least direct their thinking.

● At the end of the day, when weekly training sessions usually take place, teachers are tired. You know yourself how it feels when you have been teaching each day – it's an exhausting job. If your budget allows, bring some refreshments to your session (fruit, bagels or tempting biscuits) to lift energy levels.

● There are many books on the market to help with public speaking. *Lend Me Your Ears* by Professor Max Atkinson (Vermillion, 2004) and *Public Speaking and Presentations for Dummies* by Malcolm Kushner and Rob Yeung (John Wiley and Sons, 2006) are useful introductions.

● A warm-up activity can break the ice and be a helpful change from the day. Some fun ice-breakers can be found at www.residentassistant.com/games/icebreakers.htm and an internet search for 'ice-breakers' will give you many more. They should be no more than 5–10 minutes and should be fun. Laughter puts people into the right frame of mind and makes them open to your subject.

You Can... **Delegate**

Delegation is an important aspect of leadership; simply put, you can't do everything yourself. Good delegation can save you time and motivate colleagues who feel part of your leadership process. Poor delegation, on the other hand, can create an atmosphere of frustration, cause people to oppose you and confuse ideas, leading to jobs failing to be done. So, the ability to delegate is an essential skill to have and getting it right will enhance the success of your subject.

Thinking points

● Delegation can provide genuine professional development opportunities. If you are considering delegating a responsibility, you must first identify the person to whom it will be delegated. It may be that a handover period is required, depending on the colleague's experience. Appropriate support should be provided with clear milestones indicated.

● Delegate evenly. It is easy to fall into the trap of delegating to colleagues who are either competent or willing.

● Managing the work delegated to you, as well as the work you are able to delegate, is part of juggling middle leadership. The principles of why other people will delegate to you are the same as why you would delegate to another, such as providing an opportunity for professional development or that there is an expectation that you can get the job done well.

Tips, ideas and activities

● When delegating, it is important to define exactly what it is you are asking somebody to do. This will avoid confusion and make the task measurable.

● You will have reasons for delegating certain tasks. Typically, the more challenging tasks will be delegated to those you know best and therefore have the greatest confidence in their skills. That said, it is important to nurture new talent and you should consider why you are delegating a task and what that person is going to get out of it.

● Be aware of people's capabilities. Are they able to do the task or will they require support?

● Agree the deadline for a job. This will allow you to keep to timelines/schedules. Consider what is needed to complete the task. Will your colleague require time out of class? Ask a senior school leader if time can be arranged in order to set realistic expectations with your colleague.

● Communicate with appropriate colleagues what work needs to be done and who is doing it, which may require the School Leadership Team being informed.

● Support your colleague to enable them to complete the task.

● Review the results. This is essential for improvement.

● An easy-to-remember acronym for good delegation is SMART, or SMARTER:
  ● Specific
  ● Measurable
  ● Agreed
  ● Realistic
  ● Time-bound
  ● Ethical (could be replaced with 'Enjoyment')
  ● Recorded.

You Can... **Step up**

Good subject leaders will, inevitably, be promoted. After all, schools need to be led by the best and, in an environment where it is increasingly risky to award promotions from outside the school, you may prove to be the best candidate. Stepping up demands changes, most importantly to your time management and your relationships with colleagues. How you manage these changes will determine how successfully you can make the step up to senior levels of school management.

Thinking points

● You will, most likely, have strong views on education. How you express those views in public needs care and consideration, particularly if you do not agree with the collective school leadership. Ultimately, you are part of this team and any disagreement should be taken up before the decision has been agreed. That said, it is not always possible to raise an objection in what can be intense meetings. If you feel this has been the case then approach either the headteacher or deputy to discuss the matter further. There will be times when you do not agree with decisions made but disagreements should be kept professionally private.

● Learn to say no. Although there will be renewed expectations, sometimes they go beyond what you are capable of or have time for. Far from losing respect, you will gain respect by knowing the limits of your capabilities.

Tips, ideas and activities

● If you are new to senior school leadership ask for a mentor, ideally someone other than the headteacher. They will be able to explain how the senior leadership systems work and provide advice based on their personal experience.

● Learning how a School Leadership Team works is important to being a successful member. Although you may be keen to prove yourself, do not be rash to lead on major whole-school projects alone until you have found your feet in your new role. This can take up to a year but generally after a term you should understand the mechanics and be ready to contribute in a more significant way.

● Ask for agendas to be emailed or given to you prior to meetings. This will give you time to research, and understand, what the team will be discussing.

● Being a senior leader can be as big a change as becoming a newly-qualified class teacher. Your perspective adjusts and you should now demonstrate a holistic awareness of the whole school. With that awareness you will need to understand that your profile within the school and whole community will grow and that will include an expected change in attitude towards school leadership initiatives.

● Time will be your most precious commodity. How you manage it will be a measure of your success as a school leader. You will find you become very popular within your new role and staff will ask you for information all of the time. This can be in the most inconvenient of places, such as while you are on the run in the corridor or trying to get to the loo! It is therefore worth keeping your diary/notebook with you at all times so that comments or requests can be recorded.

You Can... # Plan for professional development for you and your colleagues

With a renewed emphasis on performance management there is an equal renewed emphasis on professional development. It has moved from being an entitlement to forming a necessary aspect of a professional career. We are smarter about what we consider professional development to involve: it is not simply isolated, individual days out at the local professional development centre, but involves a long-term view about self-change and its impact on learning.

Thinking points

● Professional development can be an experience as well as an academic exercise. Taking opportunities to visit other schools is rewarding as it offers the chance to see how another school works, which may be aside from the core purpose of the visit but is always a positive addition.

● Career development requires planning. A long-term approach to where you would like to drive your career will enable you to pace your professional development to meet your needs. It is always useful to discuss your career path with a senior colleague as your school may be able to offer support. Although a career can span several decades, three to five years is a tangible period of time to action and research the professional development you require in order to make any professional changes.

Tips, ideas and activities

● Increasingly teachers and school leaders are taking the opportunity to work overseas. Not only are they exposed to new learning environments but new cultural experiences. The British Council offers a range of opportunities through the Comenius programme. For more information visit www.britishcouncil.org/comenius.htm

● The National College for School Leadership (NCSL) runs a course aimed specifically at subject leaders called Leading from the Middle (LftM). The course runs for nine months and has a specific focus on developing leadership style. For more information visit www.ncsl.org.uk and search for the programme.

● You may be considering Advanced Skills Teacher status. Information about this can be found on the TDA's website but the position is open to all teachers, including part-time colleagues. Teachers who apply must demonstrate that they have evidence to pass all six standards and take part in a one-day assessment before AST status is granted. AST status, for experienced colleagues, is a valuable opportunity where the traditional career promotion model does not apply.

● Websites that you can access to support professional development include:
   ● http://www.tda.gove.uk/teachers continuingprofessionaldevelopment.aspx
   ● http://www.teachernet.gove.uk professionaldevelopment

You Can... Observe colleagues

Mentioning observations sends shudders down most teachers' spines. It's not that they fear they are unsatisfactory it's more that teachers are rarely observed and, as such, it can feel threatening. Most teachers want to show themselves at their best and for some reason they often feel this won't happen when being observed. It's hardly surprising when you consider in a potentially 30 year-long career where tens of thousands of lessons have been taught, it is likely that less than 30 of them will have been observed. Observation is a good thing as it tightens practice and helps identify strengths around the school.

Thinking points

A research document by the National College of School Leadership (NCSL) concluded that 'Middle leaders tend to show great resistance to the idea of monitoring the quality of their colleagues' work, especially by observing them in the classroom. Observation is seen as a challenge to professional norms of equality and privacy, and sometimes as an abrogation of trust.' (*The Role and Purpose of Middle Leaders in Schools*, 2003, NCSL, p1) However, the paper went on to demonstrate that 'Subject leaders who managed to introduce some sort of classroom observation procedure did so as a collaborative learning activity for the entire department rather than as a management activity for the subject leader.' Highlighting this aspect of observation can help to de-personalise it, making colleagues feel more confident about the process.

Tips, ideas and activities

● If you have never led an observation, ask to work with a senior colleague for your first few. This will help develop your ability to accurately assess lessons you observe.

● You don't have to observe a whole lesson. It is important to look at a specific aspect, which you can agree with the colleague you are observing.

● Plan observations as far in advance as possible and remind your colleague of the agreed date one week before the observation. Ensure that you have supply cover for that period!

● Be clear about what paperwork you expect to receive before the observation, such as copies of any resources and a lesson plan.

● You will have only limited time to conduct lesson observations. Shorter observations can allow you to observe two teachers in one period. Allow time for writing up your report. If you have a laptop you may wish to type-up notes while observing the lesson.

● When feeding back from a lesson, always ask the teacher how they felt the lesson went. Invariably they will identify the same strengths and areas for development you have.

● Aim to balance feedback with 80 per cent praise and 20 per cent areas for development.

● Be honest, but not brutally honest.

● Agree your final report with your colleague when feeding back from an observation. This gives them the opportunity to challenge any observations or time for you to clarify them.

● Give a copy of your final report to the headteacher or a senior colleague as this will form part of the evidence for the SEF.

You Can... **Listen to the children's voice**

In recent years, schools have begun the good work of actively listening to children. Most schools have a school council and many schools are beginning to involve children in higher-order tasks such as curriculum or policy development. These tasks are part of the core purpose of schools and, as children are the primary clients, it makes good sense when developing these resources that children form a central part of the consultation process.

Thinking points
● The school house system, recently popularised by the Harry Potter books, is beginning to return as a useful forum for the children's voice. It can nurture young leadership, provide a range of useful school-based tasks and offer an early introduction into the democratic system.

● Recent research conducted by Helen Bishton, on behalf of the National College for School Leadership (NCSL), concluded that what often caused negative feelings in school was relationship-driven. It is therefore important to reflect on the quality of relationships that children have with staff and peers. She also noted that children don't tend to find adults a major factor in their happiness in school and concluded that we need to listen more to the voices of children.

● Teaching children about their rights and responsibilities means they are more likely to actively challenge prejudice and injustice when they are adults rather than lack the basic skills to stand up for themselves.

Tips, ideas and activities
● Talk to children. They know your subject from the point of view of the end-user and can provide useful information on impact and content delivery, and are often candid in their views! When talking to children aim to keep your questions as open as possible. A group of four children is a good dynamic when consulting and, ideally, select groups across key stages or years.

● Depending on the focus of your subject, it may be worth involving the school council. Changes in curriculum emphasis can be explained to children by their council representatives on your behalf. Clearly identify the importance of children in your subject area.

● Not all children find they are in a position to be heard. Hard-to-reach groups should be identified by the school in order to make an effort to involve them. What makes them a hard-to-reach group may not be down to language barriers or special need. They may be shy or insecure or from a broken family. It is the school's responsibility to identify these groups if they wish to be seen as genuinely seeking the views of *all* children.

● 11 Million is an organisation led by the Children's Commissioner, Sir Al Aynsley-Green. It has a simple remit: to ensure that the adults in charge of children listen to their views. Their website is a rich resource for both children and adults: www.11million.org.uk

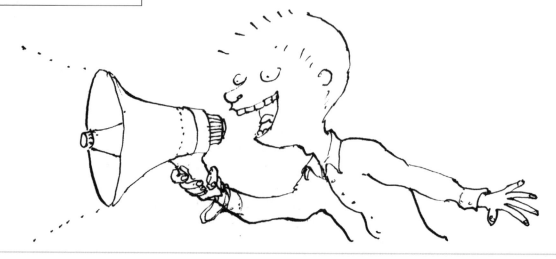

You Can... **Write a good policy**

A policy underpins your practice, what you expect from colleagues' practice and how the school community should benefit from it. It should not be personal in style but should reflect the overriding aims that the school has for a particular area and what systems it has in place for quality assurance. A good policy should be short and clearly written, with an achievable agenda.

Thinking points

● How are other members of your school community, such as parents and children, able to access your policies? Increasingly, schools are making policies available online and they must be easy to access within school (such as in central waiting areas). You should also be offering policies in the major, if not all, languages spoken in your school.

● A good policy should include:
  ○ A clear definition of the subject.
  ○ An agreed vision, objectives and action plan.
  ○ Strategies that are clear and transparent.
  ○ Reference to, and coherence with, other school policies.
  ○ A statement of support from the School Leadership Team (SLT) and governors.
  ○ A clear set of strategies you intend to implement over the coming year.
  ○ Reviewing and monitoring procedures, including a timescale for review.
  ○ Specific staff, pupil and parent responsibilities.
  ○ The date of the policy agreement, with a central copy signed by the chair of governors.

Tips, ideas and activities

● Have you involved your children in the writing of your policy? Arguably they are the people that this policy will have most impact on and yet very few schools regularly involve children when writing policies. Yes, it does add time to its development but the impact it has on children's awareness, and therefore involvement in a particular subject, will outweigh the cost of the additional time.

● Allocate enough time when writing a policy. Generally the spring term is a good time of year as you are not under pressure with report writing and you will have got to know your class well enough to begin devoting time to other areas. Be mindful that there may be a few nights in front of the computer during this process!

● Consider your language style. There is a tendency for teachers to put on their 'lawyers'' hats and write in a style that is foreign to them and outsiders. Policies should be easy to read and quick to understand. Jargon implies that there is an agenda to the policy, which is rarely the case, and can be avoided by adopting a plain-English writing style.

● Don't try to reinvent the wheel. There are plenty of online policies available (with some being better than others) that can provide a useful starting point or at least some ideas on what to include in your document.

● Evaluate your policy every year to ensure it is current or to make any necessary tweaks to bring it up to date. Once done, date it and update the appropriate communication channels (usually the school website, central resource and governors' folders).

You Can... **Evaluate planning**

Planning is arguably the backbone of good teaching. Effective planning demonstrates that a teacher is aware of the learning needs of the children in their class and the various strategies that they need to engage in order to meet them. It should identify where other adults are being directed, what resources are required and how the lesson should be adapted to meet the various levels of learning. Clear planning makes use of all the strengths of the class and avoids 'down periods'. It is no coincidence that the first 'P' in 'PPA' refers to planning; good planning is crucial when maximising learning opportunities.

Thinking points

The ICT revolution has been a great bonus to teachers, particularly when it comes to planning. With little effort, colleagues are able to produce professional planning documents that can be circulated electronically as well as physically. However, as a subject leader you should aim to have a core question in the back of your mind when evaluating these documents: does this planning meet the needs of every child in this particular class? It is too easy to produce planning that does not. Encourage colleagues to write on the plans, which not only shows that they are engaging with some form of evaluation but demonstrates that they are actively editing a document to respond to the needs of their own class.

Tips, ideas and activities

● When evaluating planning you should ask yourself a number of questions:
  ● What is it that you want from colleagues' planning?
  ● Does it meet the needs of the class?
  ● Does the planning explain how other adults are being used within the classroom?
  ● What provision is there for SEN, and gifted and talented pupils?
  ● What does the school's planning policy state and does it reflect current thinking?
  ● Are there any common themes occurring within the planning such as teachers identifying good use of adult support?
  ● How are you going to feed back to colleagues?

● Colleagues may demonstrate the same type of anxiety to a planning scrutiny as they do to lesson observations. In reality, a foundation subject may only be scrutinised two or three times a year. Consider how you could minimise this anxiety. It may be useful for phase groups, such as key stages, to review each other's planning and provide feedback to you. That said, you are ultimately responsible for the subject you lead and need to be fully aware of the standard of planning for it.

● Planning is time-consuming. The thinking point above highlights the dangers of cloned electronic planning but, if used wisely, a downloaded lesson plan can be a great time saver and provide a useful perspective on the learning objective. There are many websites available (try a quick search for 'primary planning') and some notably useful ones include:
  ● www.primaryresources.co.uk
  ● www.tlfe.org.uk
  ● www.teachingideas.co.uk
  ● www.google.co.uk/intl/en/schools/
  ● www.teachers.tv

You Can... Identify good quality schemes

What is the difference between a scheme of work and planning? In most cases it comes down to overview. Schemes of work generally take a holistic view of the whole course, which may be 12 or 13 weeks, and suggest lessons based on learning objectives. Planning involves teachers in adapting schemes to meet the needs of the class. In its simplest form, a scheme of work is a resource, albeit a tempting resource to use wholesale! This is where subject leaders must keep a careful eye on things – the scheme should meet the needs of the children and not the other way round.

Thinking points

● Consider carefully how your colleagues use published schemes of work. They should act as a resource, not dictate learning objectives or teaching styles. Ultimately, our core aim is to teach to the National Curriculum objectives. It may be that a scheme digs deeper into objectives, which can add to the rich learning experience. Equally it can overload the curriculum, as the QCA Schemes of Work did ten years ago. An inflated curriculum does not always allow learning to penetrate and teachers should keep a professional eye on 'token objectives' and use professional judgement when they feel children have met the requirement.

● A scheme of work can be a useful springboard to other ideas. Encourage teachers to keep that in mind when using one. Naturally, colleagues who are specialists will find this easier and their skills should be shared.

Tips, ideas and activities

● What is the purpose of the scheme? It may be that you are providing it to support teachers' needs and therefore it has a professional development aspect to it. If that is the case then it is useful to take feedback from colleagues who have been using it, to assess how useful they have found it and whether they feel their own practice has improved as a result.

● The internet is a great tool for teachers. It not only provides up-to-date and often exciting resources but has a wealth of international and national curricula available to download and use. As with planning (see page 20), subject leaders must check that these documents are used and adapted to meet the needs of the class and that they adhere to national standards.

● How do you evaluate your schemes? Schemes can be very expensive and if a school is considering purchasing one, then it may be worth involving a test group or the School Leadership Team when evaluating the scheme.

● Will the scheme withstand change to the curriculum? At the time of publication, Sir Jim Rose will be announcing changes to the National Curriculum. It is worth considering if your scheme will meet the national requirements or not. Equally, older schemes may well have a lot to offer – it should not be a case of throwing the baby out with the bath water but ensuring that the resource is meeting the learning needs of the class.

● Although not a paper scheme of work, Teachers TV offers a lot of advice when developing lesson plans. Teachers can download a wide range of resources and access 15-minute video clips from the Teachers TV website: www.teachers.tv

● Some useful schemes of work can be found on the following websites:
  ○ www.standards.dcsf.gov.uk
  ○ www.teachernet.gov.uk (search for 'schemes of work')
  ○ www.nacell.org.uk (search for 'schemes of work')

You Can... Get the best from your children

Children are what this job is all about. Their enthusiasm for learning, abundance of energy and excitement make teaching dynamic and ever-changing. Getting the best from them meets your core purpose and creates better harmony between you and those 30 or so individuals. This can be challenging and tiring, but if done properly it is the most satisfying experience going!

Thinking points

● Communicate clearly with parents/carers to foster a co-teaching partnership between the family and yourself. This can be done by being present with the class at the end or start of the day. The children will feel more secure when in school and more accountable for their own learning. Home-school diaries are a more mature way of communicating with the home and, increasingly, printing companies are presenting schools with sophisticated home-learning journals. Investing in a quality product states that you are expecting a certain level of commitment from the child and family.

● Your children are individuals and as such will have their own strengths, which you need to uncover. Nurturing these talents may bear the most incredible fruit in their future, which you may never see.

● Differentiating is time-consuming but it can be the difference between a child feeling they can succeed or not.

Tips, ideas and activities

● It is important to get your classroom appearance right. How you design your classroom and how you decorate it reflects the type of learning environment you want to provide for your class. Remember that furniture does not need to be static. Foremost, keep your classroom clean and clutter free.

● Children can create a huge amount of mess and should be responsible for tidying up after themselves. They can only do this if there are systems in place for putting things away. Clearly labelling drawers, cupboards and table-tops is a job worth doing as it will save time in your daily routines.

● Aim for a mix of pupil and commercially-produced displays. Although commercially-produced displays can look glossy and have all the right information, if the children don't have any work alongside it they will be less likely to interact with the resource. Equally, aim to rotate displays at least every term. This keeps the learning current and is a statement that says you value your children's work.

● Use positive reward systems; praise good behaviour as well as work. Create team pressure by awarding groups with merit points. Also praise the whole class if you have had a good morning. Working towards an agreed goal is a great incentive.

● Always be clear with your learning intentions. If the children know what you are expecting them to produce then they are far more likely to understand how to do it.

You Can... **Assess pupil progress**

It has been clear for a number of years that children across the country have reached a plateau with their overall attainment. National and local data showed that a significant number of pupils have not been making satisfactory progress during a key stage, with some pupils becoming 'stuck' or, even worse, regressing during some stages in their education. An assessment procedure was needed to take a close look at which specific areas children were failing in. As such, Assessing Pupils' Progress (APP) was launched in a number of local authorities in 2008, with a national launch in September 2009.

Thinking points

The Assessment Focuses laid out in the APP guidelines are more detailed than the objectives found in the renewed Primary Framework. In some ways, they are similar to the objectives used by the original literacy and numeracy strategies. This has raised a question about depth of coverage and whether the renewed strategies are able to drill down as far as the APP requires.

Tips, ideas and activities

● APP uses Assessment Focuses (AFs) to cover periodic assessment. AFs are drawn from the National Curriculum and sit alongside the level descriptors and learning objectives. These focuses can be linked to the objectives and can help pace your assessment during the year.

● Setting up your first APP file requires commitment. If it is your first experience of using the APP approach then focus on three children at different levels of ability (high, secure and low). Create a folder for each child. Evidence collected can be placed into the folders.

● APP requires planning over the year. If you have another adult in the room, you can direct them to observe your target children in order to gather evidence against the Assessment Focuses.

● Evidence can be collected in a number of ways, many of which are common practice in the Foundation Stage. Sticky notes, photographs, observations, book work and formal tests are all useful pieces of evidence. If your school has a Foundation Stage then it is worth visiting them to see how they collect their evidence and how it is used in relation to the Early Years objectives.

● The Standards website will support your school's roll out of APP. Visit www.standards.dcsf.gov.uk, select 'Primary Framework', then choose 'Assessment'.

● ICT leaders should find this site of use: http://tlfe.org.uk/ict/assessingict

You Can... Include other cultures and languages

Britain is a very culturally diverse country. One London borough has an estimated 196 languages with many of its schools supporting 30 or more languages. But this is not uncommon within our inner cities. Learning how to get the best from this culturally-rich resource is a challenge for schools and particularly for individual teachers who are at the front line. But it is a resource and brings real meaning to the term 'global village', which just happens to be in many of our classrooms.

Thinking points

● The internet has done much to highlight the importance of world cultures and language. Although it is dominated by English vocabulary, websites in other languages, such as Arabic, French and traditional Chinese, are quickly growing in number. Intelligent programs that can translate language are making it much easier for web designers to create one site and have it available in any number of languages. Far from being the end of cultures, as was originally feared, it is a forum where they are thriving.

● The Welsh Assembly has been proactive in supporting Welsh-language resources in schools. In 2002 they introduced the Welsh Baccalaureate for sixth formers with a long-term view that it could replace A-levels in the future. It is a strong example of language regeneration in our modern, English-dominated culture.

Tips, ideas and activities

● Make your classroom a language-rich environment. For children who are unfamiliar with English, seeing words in their language with the English equivalent will help to reinforce basic vocabulary. A good website to start with is http://the-treasure-box.co.uk/freeresources.aspx but there are many more available.

● The internet offers a range of language translation websites such as Babel Fish (http://babelfish.yahoo.com). These sites are good at translating individual words but are not necessarily as reliable with large pieces of text because they give a literal translation rather than a sympathetic translation.

● You should know the breakdown of ethnicity within your classroom. Children who are new to learning English will have their language acquisition monitored annually (this generally takes place in late autumn). Many schools use the Hilary Hester Stages of Learning (www.clpe.co.uk/pdf/StagesofEnglishLearning.pdf). If a child does not increase in ability, strategies will be needed to support their language learning.

● Encourage children to write in their home language and display other language work alongside English equivalents. This will build confidence. Equally, support parents in speaking to their children in their home language as this will keep it fresh.

● Black History Month in October is ideal for raising the awareness of black achievement in your school. Useful resources can be found at the following websites:
  ○ www.norfolkblackhistorymonth.org.uk
  ○ www.black-history-month.co.uk

● By 2010 it will be statutory for all schools to provide lessons in a modern foreign language. It is likely that your school will provide one lesson a week, however languages require practice. Try to fit in a ten-minute daily session such as singing songs or practising phrases in that language.

You Can... **Communicate with parents and carers**

Schools have changed dramatically for today's parents and carers, more so than when their parents were in school. Computers have taken over classrooms and the curriculum is now full of jargon that their children are comfortable with but may be an alien language to them. Making the classroom and school an inviting place for parents is as much your responsibility as it is for making it inviting for their children. Ultimately the significant adult in a child's life can help bring out the best in them at school when they understand and feel comfortable within that establishment. This includes your subject area.

Thinking points

● The Leading Parent Partnership Award (LPPA) is a Kitemark that Ofsted recognises. The award is given to schools that have demonstrated, from an agreed action plan, a significant level of parental partnership. The action plan embraces all aspects of school life from school administration to senior leadership and the classroom. It is a considerable piece of work as it demands involvement from the governors, school leaders and all class teachers but its long-term rewards outweigh this. The award, like Healthy Schools, must be renewed every three years to prove an ongoing commitment to parent involvement.

● Consider how and where you are communicating with your parents. If you are leading an event, have you displayed it on the community board or run an assembly on it or written a fun letter? This is not always necessary but enthusiasm is needed to make an event successful.

Tips, ideas and activities

● Write to your parents termly informing them about what is happening in the coming weeks in your class. Adding photographs to your letters brings them alive and gives your families valuable insight into your classroom.

● Schools are beginning to broaden their communications with parents and carers. Increasingly texting and emailing are being used to reach a broader range of people. It is a modern phenomenon that emails or texts are more likely to be read than the letter at the bottom of a child's book bag. This is also a useful way of advertising a focus event and a planned series of short emails over a period of time can be more effective than one longer letter home.

● Arranging day or evening events when parents can work alongside children in class is a valuable way of allowing children to 'shine' with their parents. It also demonstrates how day-to-day lessons work, particularly if there is a subject focus.

● Talk to parents at the start or end of the day. This allows you time to address small issues and to get to know your community, which may be useful in the future.

● Your school, particularly if it is an urban one, is likely to have a significant community language within it. Identifying this language and communicating in it, either through an interpreter or in writing, demonstrates a degree of commitment from the school. If you are planning an event then it is worth considering that a translated letter might take a number of weeks to complete. A member of your community may be able to translate the letter on your behalf.

You Can... **Report to governors**

UK schools are unique in having a governance system at the heart of school leadership. Governors tend to be silent workers, securing systems in the background and acting as the backbone to the school system. They are the critical friend who asks those challenging questions, not to intimidate but to seek clarification. The dynamics of a well-run School Leadership Team supported by a knowledgeable governing body can be impressive and are central to an effective school.

Thinking points

- Governors have three key tasks:
  1. To provide strategic vision by setting the school's aims, polices and targets.
  2. To act as a critical friend and challenge, where appropriate.
  3. To be accountable, including raising standards and managing the school's budget.

All of these tasks are undertaken in partnership with the school and the advice its leadership provides.

- Your governors may well want to visit you in school. Any visits will be fed back to the whole governing body. Prepare for the visit and keep your language as clear as possible. Although your governor will be familiar with how schools work and with many of the acronyms, do not take this for granted. A clear message from you will greatly improve the chances of a clear message being relayed back to the whole governing body.

Tips, ideas and activities

- Know your audience when talking to governors as they are not trained educators. Explain acronyms when used and try not to bulldoze your way through a report, particularly verbal, in an attempt to look like you know what you are talking about. They are there to support and can only do so when they have a clear understanding of what you are telling them.

- When you are called to give information to the governors, ensure you are giving the information they are looking for. If you are supplying any facts or figures ensure that you explain the background to your evidence and why you have submitted it with any report. Remember to agree times for meetings. It is not always possible for governors to meet during the day and both parties should be flexible for each other's needs.

- If a common set of reports, such as end-of-year subject leader reports, are requested use a common report framework with writer's guidelines. This continuity will support governors understanding of the school's work. If you haven't written one before, ask an experienced colleague to act as a mentor.

- In order to raise or maintain standards, schools need to evaluate core groups such as gender or ethnicities. It is the governors' duty to ensure that this happens. You should be prepared for some hard questioning.

- The governors and School Leadership Team are a partnership. Getting to know the governors, inviting them to visit you in class or for a meeting to update them on your areas of responsibility, are useful ways of solidifying this important relationship.

- The websites below provide information both for and about governors:
  - www.governornet.co.uk
  - www.parentscentre.gov.uk
  - www.teachernet.gov.uk

You Can... **Liaise with other agencies**

The school community has broadened over the last few years and, with the growing relationship with children's centres, it is due to continue expanding in the coming decade. Simply put, schools are no longer lone beacons and, increasingly, new services are working alongside teachers to support the children and families that they serve. Schools are becoming part of multi-agency teams which include health and social services and your personal experience may well be that you have a child who is supported by an educational psychologist or a speech and language therapist.

Thinking points

In an increasingly inclusive environment you are more likely to be working with other agencies that in any other educational period. Children with identified needs (or multiple needs) will be supported by a range of professionals. Having an agreed communication structure will not only support you but all of those involved with the child. The Common Assessment Framework (CAF) is a key part of delivering front line services that are integrated and focused around the needs of children and young people. The CAF is a standardised approach for conducting an assessment of a child's additional needs and deciding how those needs should be met. It can be used by practitioners across children's services in England.

Tips, ideas and activities

● Early identification of children who have a particular need is important. Your Special Educational Needs Coordinator (SENCO) will be able to support you when you are identifying what need and what level of special educational need a child is placed at, whether it is school action, school action+ or a statement.

● Once a child has been identified as having a special educational need this will trigger a range of intervention programmes to help meet the child's need. In many cases this may include an additional adult in your room for some or all of the day. It is your role to manage the support by having clear objectives, a timetable of support and by clearly informing everyone who is involved with the child, including the carers. This will support your overall management of the class.

● Over 3000 children's centres will be created by 2011. These centres will offer a wide range of services that families with young children (below five years old) can access. Many of these centres will be connected to schools and bring external services directly into the school, such as family support workers and health services. In these cases schools, as partners with a children's centre, will have access to any services provided and more opportunity to liaise with teams who are usually external to the site. This will allow the teacher and SENCO, who have identified a need (such as speech and language), to act far more quickly than at present.

● In all likelihood you will have children each year who come to your class with some level of special need. Your school will most likely have a handover period in July for you to liaise with the existing teacher. It is important to find out who has additional need, what that need entails and if external agencies are already used to support that child.

You Can... **Use your community**

Schools are going through a change. Ten years ago it was the curriculum that was its principle focus and while that remains a school's core purpose, the spotlight has moved direction and is now shining out into the community. More and more schools are seeing exciting ways of developing new partnerships within their community. When effective, these partnerships are providing an enriched learning experience for the children within the community and a new set of resources upon which the school can draw.

Thinking points

● The Wisconsin Department of Public Instruction (http://dpi.wi.gov) has helpfully identified four key reasons to support school/ community partnerships. They are universal goals that we should all be working towards:

1. When parents, teachers, students, and others view one another as knowledgeable partners in education, a caring community forms around students.
2. Partnerships should be an integral part of the school's regular work.
3. Students learn and grow at home, at school, and in their communities.
4. The best predictor of a student's achievement in school is not income or social status, but the extent to which the student's family is able to:
   ● Create a home environment that encourages learning;
   ● Communicate high, yet reasonable, expectations for their children's achievement and future careers;
   ● Become involved in their children's education at home, at school, and in the community.

Tips, ideas and activities

● Getting the community into school can be challenging. Themed events, such as RE weeks or history days, are ideal opportunities for seeking out experts within the community.

● For a specific event you may wish to consider writing to your school community. If you are trying to identify gardeners (if you are the sustainability leader) or historians, they are more likely to come forward if they know who to approach and feel as if the school has invited them in.

● Rural schools have worked at developing closer links with community leaders for many years. The Rural School and Community Trust (www.ruraledu.org) was established for this very reason: to support rural schools and communities working together.

● INSPIRE events can be an excellent way to bring parents and carers into school. To run an INSPIRE event you should:
   ● Focus on one year group at a time.
   ● Invite a significant adult to work with each child in the class/es (this could include other teachers around the school).
   ● Organise the event to take place in one afternoon or morning as this is often easier for adults to take time off work. Keep the event secret but it could be DT-based (making masks), a writing event, designing maths games but should be something that the child and adult can do together.
   ● Ensure you have all the resources needed for the event.
   ● Take photographs of and comments from everyone involved during the event
   ● Celebrate the event in an assembly with the adults who have been involved and give each person their own certificate.

You Can... Identify need and support colleagues

Need and support are generally linked. Being able to identify a need, be it professional development or resource demand, ultimately leads to supporting an individual colleague. It is where leading a subject shifts from school-wide guidance to micro-leadership. Understanding an individual's needs demonstrates a school's commitment to colleagues and individualised learning at all levels.

Thinking points

● Examining planning can raise questions particularly if little adaptation has been made or the roles of additional adults have not been identified. Modern planning can look very professional but looks can be deceiving and you should be examining it for evidence that every child is being catered for. Where this is not happening it could be an indicator of a lack of teacher confidence in the subject, which could be supported by professional development either internally or externally.

● Teaching is a busy job and where we can find time-saving devices, they should be promoted. No doubt you will have your own set of time-savers but a new colleague or NQT might need support when managing the workload. Support should not be imposed, but an offer of help is generally accepted.

Tips, ideas and activities

● Although it could be argued that resources don't automatically lead to learning there is little doubt that appropriate resources help. They give teachers the tools of the trade, which makes them more confident in their practice. An audit of resource need is best done at the start of the academic year when the overview of curriculum is fresh in people's minds.

● Asking colleagues to write down their resource needs for your subject at the start of a staff meeting should take no more than 15 minutes and could fit into a start-of-term training day.

● Be clear with colleagues that your budget is limited so that this at least gives them the opportunity to either request exact resources or identify areas where they need additional support, which will makes them feel part of the procurement process. Equally, resources are more likely to be used if requested rather than imposed. The staff will feel confident that they will have the resources they need in good time and it gives you a concrete piece of work to do that is meeting direct need.

● Ask colleagues what resources they are using. Good resources get passed round the staff room quickly and should be shared. If your school has a central communications board then use it to advertise a useful resource or 'website of the month' to share with colleagues. Remember to indicate who found it to give them the credit!

● Establishing ways to identify need, particularly if it is professional development, requires communication. The School Leadership Team and phase leaders can act as your eyes and ears when identifying need across the school.

SCHOOL SUPPLIES 'R' US

You Can... **Develop teaching assistants**

In the last five years a virtual army of teaching assistants (TAs) have been recruited into primary schools across the country. Their use within schools varies depending on the need of the establishment, but what has significantly changed is their profile. Gone are the days when TAs would do the photocopying or display mounting. Today a TA's core purpose is teaching and being a co-teacher within the classroom. This has resulted in improved professional development, performance management and raised expectations.

Thinking points

Everyone who works in a school has a part to play in raising standards and giving pupils a better start in life. As a result, TAs should expect to receive appropriate professional development from the time they start working. Introductory training helps new TAs and support staff to understand their role, feel confident in their work and be effective members of the school team. Longer-serving staff will also find it useful as a refresher to bring them up to date with policies and practice. Involving TAs in Continuing Professional Development (CPD) programmes alongside teachers will ensure that all the adults in classrooms are aware of current practice and are working towards a common purpose.

Tips, ideas and activities

● Consider your communication with the TAs in your class. What strategies have you in place so that they know what you are intending to teach and how you intend to differentiate it? If possible, involve your TA in part or all of your planning sessions (during PPA time) so that they have an overall view of the short-term plans.

● Clearly timetable how you use your TA as there may be other adults who are involved with your children during the week who come from other services such as Educational Psychologists or Behaviour Support. Keeping your timetable clear and well displayed will help you, the class and the other adults who are with you stay informed.

● How are the TAs utilised within your school for your subject? It may be that one of your TAs has a particular skill, such as sports or music. It is possible to re-grade a TA to include a specialism within their job description, equivalent to a teacher's TLR point.

● TAs, through the workforce remodelling changes in 2003, now have a career structure that includes higher level teaching assistants. It is seen by many as a way into schools and many colleges now offer courses on how to be a Teaching Assistant. The Training and Development Agency for Schools (TDA) has created a 'career development framework' to support TAs when considering a potential career pathway. It identifies progression opportunities within and across different occupational roles in the school workforce. More information about the framework can be found on the TDA website, www.tda.gov.uk (search for 'career development framework').

You Can... **Work with action groups or teams**

People enjoy being in teams and nowhere is this more apparent than in a school. Teachers are, by nature, sociable creatures. Teams can give purpose to, and increase enthusiasm about, a subject or theme and this, in turn, is infectious. The sum of a team's work can be greater than the work of the number of individuals involved. It is also a clear indicator that someone is valued by inviting them onto a team and that the school view this as a high priority by investing the time in creating the group.

Thinking points
● Over the last five years, schools have employed tens of thousands of teaching assistants (TAs). Many of these are highly qualified individuals in their own right and all will certainly bring a range of skills to the school. It is important to consider the use of this talented resource. Some schools have begun to establish shadow leadership structures where TAs are allocated to work alongside subject leaders, adding to the subject's skill set and providing an additional set of hands.

● Teams need a clear goal otherwise they risk becoming stale. For this reason expect teams to have a clear focus each year (this may be created by the team or be provided by the SLT) and for the teams to be reshuffled occasionally. This keeps ideas fresh and the focus on what children need at that present time.

Tips, ideas and activities
● Teams do not need to be large. You might have just one other person who acts as your shadow. It is an opportunity to act as a mentor if this colleague is new to your subject.

● Agree when you are going to meet as a team and for how long. Keeping to a strict time frame will keep your meeting tight and will also acknowledge that colleagues have busy lives.

● Teams provide a useful forum for delegating tasks that you would normally have to undertake yourself. Use the team for this purpose as you will be able to achieve more, which will increase activity across the school.

● Teams generally require a lead spokesperson; somebody who is managing the teams' action. If it is a team that you have established then this will naturally fall to you.

● Teams can reflect the school's community by involving teaching staff, parents, children and governors. What must be considered, when creating a broad spectrum group, is your use of language. It is good practice to use plain English in public forums. An agreed, clear understanding of any action is vital when driving your subject forward.

● Communication is important, particularly with colleagues outside of your team. You may have good written skills but another colleague may be more confident when addressing the School Leadership Team or governors. Use your colleagues' strengths to the team's collective advantage.

● Celebrate success. Go out for a meal or a drink after work as a team. Success often brings more success and it is important to enjoy the moment.

You Can... **Work with the local media**

Working with the local media, such as local radio or newspaper, is becoming more common with middle leaders. Increasingly it is the middle leaders who have something to say that is of local interest, such as a science week, international day or Yellow Pages recycling scheme. As you would be the champion of this newsworthy project, it makes sense that you should be responsible for publicising it – and why not? If you are doing something that is unique, fun or interesting, the local community may want to know about it.

Thinking points

● Local authorities will have a communications team. Generally speaking, any statements, advertising or public announcements should be run past them first. It is a useful policy to have as it protects the school. That said, don't be afraid to bend the rules a little bit if time is against you and the school has agreed to your action.

● Good relations with the local press will generally mean that they will be predisposed to 'run' your story. Equally if there is negative news it means that you may have a strategic ally. Your school may have a communications policy that includes how to talk to journalists. Whether it has a policy or not, it is important to be aware that local newspapers support the local community and are not out to trick you into disclosure. They want good relations with a school that can provide regular, community-based stories.

Tips, ideas and activities

● Aim to identify a newsworthy event as soon as possible, giving time to arrange how you would like it communicated. From a media point of view, spring is a good time to run events, such as a curriculum evening or week, as it picks up from the December festivals and isn't jostling for space with summer fairs. Your event may require just a photographer. A good photograph can often be as effective as an article.

● Your school should have a children's photograph permission letter (often these are attached to induction papers that you may not be aware of). If you are not sure or if the event is a significantly large one, then it is courtesy to inform families that their child may be photographed. On these occasions it is useful to write an opt-out letter where parents have to inform the school that they do not want their child photographed rather than informing the school that they do.

● As the organiser of the event it would be reasonable to expect that you may have to write the press release. When writing a statement, use a simple writing style that describes what the event is, who is involved, when it is happening and why it is happening. Do not embellish. Ask a senior colleague, such as the headteacher or deputy/assistant headteacher, to proofread the statement before releasing it.

● Know who your local newspapers are and ask which have been supportive of the school in the past. Being able to say to a journalist that they have been recommended is a friendly way of opening your conversation.

● If your school is at the edge of boroughs, which is not uncommon in urban areas, you may want to consider approaching newspapers that fall just outside of your borough.

You Can... Manage your time for a work/life balance

Although teachers enjoy 13 weeks of holiday a year, when you are at work you work hard. Managing your time and setting realistic goals is vital in order to obtain a reasonable work/life balance, which if left unguarded can be eroded away. Spending more hours in front of a PC or at the chalk face does not necessarily equal better productivity. It can lead to burnout, apathy and antipathy towards the workplace. Ring-fenced time out of class, such as PPA or management time, was introduced in 2005 to support teachers and was an important step towards acknowledging the challenge of juggling the class, school/subject leadership and home life.

Thinking points

● There is a saying that we should 'work to live, not live to work'. In many cases it is a fair one, however it is inevitable that when you take on more responsibility your workload will increase.

● If you are struggling with your workload, talk to a line manager or your headteacher. They may not be aware of your position and will, in all likelihood, be able to provide support and encouragement.

● The school life has a natural cycle and there are periods of time that are tougher than others (typically it is more challenging at the end of term, as an example). If you have mapped out the year and measured the lengths of each term then it is easier to pace your work life.

Tips, ideas and activities

● Set challenging, but realistic goals. When you overstretch yourself this is ultimately to the detriment of your class. They need a healthy teacher who is clear-headed.

● Use a diary. It is quite obvious but a diary will help you manage your life during those precious periods between lessons.

● Learn to say no. As teachers we naturally gravitate towards new ideas but there are only so many initiatives we can manage at once. Saying no does not mean that something or someone is not valued, it is managing a situation – you know your limits.

● Use the systems within your school to support your working week. These systems should highlight upcoming events, such as Continuing Professional Development (CPD) or when tasks need to be completed. See pages 57 to 59 for a suggested timetable of core events that will impact on your leadership.

● Be prepared. If your teaching time is well prepared then your lessons will run smoothly. Clear and concise objectives will support a well-run lesson.

● As well as having a clear curriculum timetable it is worth establishing clear roles and responsibilities within the classroom that the children can manage themselves.

● Inform parents when you are available to meet them and let them know when you are away from the class. They are then informed of any change to the teacher, why it's happening and what the global benefits are for the school.

You Can... **Audit skills and resources**

It wasn't that long ago that if someone mentioned an 'audit' it simply meant a stock-taking exercise with the subject coordinator running round the school in half a day with a clipboard ticking off what resources the school did or did not have. It was, in its crudest form, a management task and all it told the coordinator was what resources the teachers had there and then to lead teaching. Today, subject leaders should be looking to complete an audit of skills – the potential human resources that are available to the school for ongoing, future learning.

Thinking points

● Physical resources are very useful and often vital to make a learning experience come alive. However, they should not be the stumbling block that prevents lessons taking place. With the advent of the internet and interactive whiteboards teachers, arguably, have a limitless range of virtual resources if the genuine article is not available.

● Use any audit to help shape and plan your subject's future in partnership with the school's vision. If a subject begins to stray away from the school's vision/ethos it risks a certain amount of vulnerability and becomes reliant on the particular individual who is leading it. Future-proofing occurs when robust systems are in place with a shared understanding of the subject's core purposes.

Tips, ideas and activities

● Identify the skills you are attempting to audit. It may be that you are aiming to make a baseline assessment, such as identifying the modern foreign languages spoken by your staff, or you may be looking for expertise. Part of the role of the subject leader is to identify which colleagues can be 'champions' for your subject.

● What is the school's vision for learning? If it is to embed digital technologies across the curriculum, use that as a basis for your skills and resources audit.

● Identify your local resource centres, such as libraries or specialist schools, and raise their profile within school. Lending libraries or artefact centres require a certain amount of administration, which could be shared by all the staff. Your role is to act as a facilitator for this resource and to keep it active.

● Human resources can also be shared between schools. Lead teachers and coaches are available for one-off or short-term use between schools.

● Build a working relationship with the local subject consultant. Although most foundation subjects no longer have a local authority designated individual, there are usually plenty of people who are available to offer good advice, particularly if you are new to your area of responsibility.

● It is worth auditing your local community for experts. Many parents are very happy to work in schools or share their skills. This does not always have to be in classes. For example, a keen parent gardener can be invaluable when supporting any allotment projects. Often a letter home can uncover enthusiastic carers who are experts in their field.

You Can... **Manage a budget**

Budgets vary across departments, from year to year and between schools. The one thing that defines them all is that you can only spend what you've got! How you spend your budget, particularly if it is a small one, can be challenging, as there are few cases where people have enough money for everything they want. It's a balancing act of purchasing what the staff feel they need to deliver their lessons while getting the best value for money.

Thinking points

● It is often the case that a budget holder does not have enough money in their budget. So, is there an argument for second-hand products? Given the current climate of sustainability there is added weight to consider used resources but, ultimately, if somebody does not want that resource any more (it may be an old guitar or computer) it is usually because it is past its life expectancy. Used resources send out a potentially negative message and unless it is a quality used product then the subject leader should consider its use very carefully before accepting the 'gift'.

● There is, arguably, an even stronger debate for providing children with top-quality resources if we are want to expect top-quality learning leading to top-quality results.

Tips, ideas and activities

● You should know your previous and current budgets. It is unlikely that your next budget will go down (unless there have been special circumstances surrounding it) and this will help you plan for your coming year.

● Monitor your budget. You should keep a section of your subject leader's file for finance where any invoices, order forms and receipts are kept. Your School Leadership Team has the right to ask to view how you are monitoring your budget and will expect you to give clear answers.

● If you are aware that, in the coming academic year, your subject area will have good reason for an inflated budget you will need to make this recommendation to the headteacher in March so that it can be calculated into the new budget if it is agreed.

● Be mindful that any surplus in your budget should be spent by mid-February. Your school's financial administrator will want to close the current financial year's books with all orders paid for in line with the accounting period. If you have not done this and not communicated clearly to the main budget controllers then you may lose some of your new budget if you have invoices that overlap into the new year.

● Your school may not be in a position to increase your budget. If this is the case then you might consider approaching charities (with the headteacher's consent) such as a school/parent association to sponsor individual items. Larger grants can be accessed through Awards For All or the Big Lottery Fund. It is also worth noting that some banking associations will match any money fundraised by a school for a specific resource, such as new staging.

You Can... **Manage people**

Managing people takes skill and empathy, a combination now commonly referred to as emotional intelligence. This was championed by Daniel Goleman, who generally concluded that the more complex the situation, the more emotional intelligence is required. Michael Fullan (2001) takes this one step further by explaining that 'the most effective leaders are not the smartest in an IQ sense but are those who combine intellectual brilliance with emotional intelligence'.

Thinking points

● There are various teams within schools: subject teams comprised of colleagues with a similar interest; leadership teams comprised of an upper hierarchy of school leadership; and class teams comprised of a range of adults including teaching assistants, teachers and volunteers. It is this last group that you will have day-to-day contact with and will require your daily management. Having a clear awareness of these people's individual strengths will help you to delegate responsibilities appropriately.

● Defining your team – be it class, leadership or subject – will shape it. It provides a purpose for the group of adults working together. Having a shared understanding or purpose is vital as a team that lacks this is less likely to perform well.

Tips, ideas and activities

● What strategies do you use when managing people? A good manager will use a range, but whatever strategy you use (be it autocratic, participative or delegator – see page 8 for details) consider what impact it is having and who it is benefiting. Ultimately good management guides adults and learners towards a shared goal.

● People generally need a motivation to be managed. In class this can be clear directions and when it is a whole-school project it can be a clear outcome such as planning a theme week or display theme.

● Praise success when work has been done well. This recognition raises expectation while highlighting what is good.

● Clearly communicating between adults, either using books, notes (see page 60 for a useful photocopiable resource to support communication with other adults in your classroom) or in meetings will work towards ensuring that children have a coherent learning experience from all the adults involved.

● How aware are you of your colleagues' welfare? It is not possible to support an individual if you are not aware they need support, so what strategies do you have in place to ensure that individual need is not overlooked? When working towards a common goal it is important to have an honest relationship with colleagues as the children's needs will not be met if there are barriers. Good communication, shared planning and socially spending time together will reinforce relationships. If a barrier has been created that you feel you are not able to unblock, then you must communicate this to a senior leader, who should be able to offer support.

● There are many books available that discuss how teams can work effectively, including:
  ○ *Teambuilding Activities Pocketbook* by Paul Tizzard and Phil Hailstone (Management Pocketbooks, 2006).
  ○ *Managing Teams for Dummies* by Marty Brounstein (John Wiley and Sons, 2002).

You Can... Use ICT

ICT is one of the most complex and fun aspects of modern teaching. Interactive whiteboards (wonderfully referred to by a wise headteacher as 'overactive whiteboards') have popped up in almost every classroom in the country together with a mind-boggling array of other resources including digital cameras, MP3 players, webcams and the wonderfully rich internet. The modern teacher is a light year away from what current parents remember from their school days. Today is a period of quick learning and exciting gadgets that will soon be the mainstay of all classrooms.

Thinking points

Any resource needs time to be understood, whether it is a computer program or a physical classroom resource. The temptation, however, with a computer program is to try to invest too much time learning how it works. Yes, a level of competency is needed so that it will do what you want it to do but rarely will you need to know every minor detail or keyboard shortcut to deliver a successful lesson. Knowing this, computer companies are now increasingly designing programs that are more intuitive. Ultimately they want you to use their resources but if they require a maths degree they will simply not be used. Bear this in mind when using a new resource. You know your limits and if you feel the resource is asking more than you can manage then don't use it – there will be a better one out there somewhere.

Tips, ideas and activities

● Digital cameras are a wonderful resource for recording anything from science experiments to school visits. Your school should have a parent policy that asks if photographs can be taken for school use. If you are not sure if this policy exists, then ask. Photographs have been used for gathering evidence in the Foundation Stage for many years and there is no reason why this good practice should not be reflected across the school when it comes to PE, art, science experiments, maths investigations, PSHE lessons, visiting guests. The list could go on.

● The internet is a wonderful thing and there are few days where this resource is not accessed by teachers at some time or another, be it to support learning or to find resources. When searching the internet for images or websites, try not to be too choosey when finding the perfect site. You would never have been so choosey when using a book in the past and a lot of time can be wasted this way.

● If you ask the children in your class, most of them will have an MP3 player of some kind. Apple® dominates this market and the new iPod® Touch series is set to create a new wave of digital products that are destined for the classroom and home. The interactivity of these devices mimics the class whiteboard and, in good time, most resources available to a teacher on the whiteboard will be available on these devices.

● Laptops are not yet particularly common in classrooms but it is highly likely that as production costs keep falling, they will become more present. Ten years ago most children would not have had access to computers at home whereas today they are commonplace. Schools will have to reflect this access in the classroom if they are going to meet the needs of 21st century children.

You Can... Use the school grounds as a resource

One of the most defining aspects of all schools is their site. Parents will often decide on where to send their children based on what physical resources the school has to offer. Equally for teachers it can be a key aspect that impacts on their professional life. Given that many of our schools are over 100 years old, it is exciting news that the Government is committed to spending money on these lovely old buildings. However, how you use your site is up to how creative you wish to be and a site is as much a responsibility of each member of the school as it is the headteacher's.

Thinking points

● View your school grounds as you would view your classroom. How can you get the best out of it? What does it offer? What could it offer if the school were able to adapt play spaces? They need not be the sole arenas for sport, as shelters can be built to create outside learning spaces and used much in the same way as in the Foundation Stage.

● A shared responsibility is the use of energy within school. At home you would not leave external doors open in the winter yet this is not uncommon in schools. Equally you would not keep unwanted electrical appliances on as we know they use energy. Taking the same care in school as you would at home will save the school money that can be better spent in other areas.

Tips, ideas and activities

● Identify areas that could be developed, in consultation with the headteacher. This is the first step towards building an outside stage (a roman theatre will make links with history) or a place for cycle storage (linking it to your sustainability plan).

● There must be external as well as internal play space in the Foundation Stage. This idea can be replicated around the school and certainly into Year 1. Children learn in a variety of ways and, for some children, performing the same activity outside may be the way they learn best.

● Building an environmental classroom could be as simple as converting an existing shelter in to a permanent outside learning space for all children.

● What resources do the other local schools have? Schools are generally looking to develop relationships with local partners and if another school has a really good pond, for example, then it would be worth cultivating a relationship if one does not already exist.

● The school grounds have many uses, including storage for vehicles. If your school is within London you will be eligible for free bicycle shelters if it has been specified within your school travel plan.

● Changing how the site is used is costly. However schools are able to access a range of grant bodies for large awards. These include Awards for All, the Foyle Foundation, National Sports Foundation and the British Council. An internet search for any of these will quickly lead to their individual websites, which include information about how to apply.

You Can... **Create a clear subject leader file**

A subject leader's file is their bible. It contains the essence of what they are doing, what they plan to do as well as their budget and assessment information. It is often a highly personal document. However, it is also a professional document that should be accessible to all and should have a clear system. Ultimately Her Majesty's Inspectorate for Education (HMI) would expect a subject leader to use their file as part of their discussions about the standards of their subject. The clearer the file, the smoother this process will be.

Thinking points

● In the same way that we inspect classroom planning, subject leadership files are increasingly coming under the same amount of internal scrutiny. This is for many good reasons: it can identify good practice (which in turn can be shared among the staff); it can help track action during the year; it can reinforce common practice, which leads to ease of access; and it raises professional accountability of subject leaders.

● Increasingly subject leaders will have a set of files on their computer that either complement or are a copy of their paper file. This is a useful practice as electronic paperwork is easy to distribute and quick to access. However, that said, it is always good practice to have a paper copy of core documents, such as your improvement plan, to safeguard against file corruption and to enable quick access when a computer isn't available. Although computers are useful, a flick through the file can often be as fast as searching the hard drive to print off a copy.

Tips, ideas and activities

● A file should have a common index across the school for ease of access and agreed systems. Suggested titles for an index include:
   ● Subject Improvement Plan (see page 61 for a photocopiable template).
   ● Budget.
   ● Audit of skills.
   ● Resource audit.
   ● Lesson observations.
   ● Assessment.
   ● Letters.
   ● Governors' briefing.
   ● Staff professional development.
   ● Subject policy.

● Ask yourself a key question 'Would another person be able to use this file if I were not here?' If the answer is 'no', take action to improve your file!

● HMI will, at some point in your career, inspect the standards of your subject. A clear file will support this process and make life a lot easier.

You Can... Support the school vision

Your school may have adopted a whole-school vision. It will certainly have a set of aims to which it adheres. A good vision fastens together a school's values and aims with the community's dreams for tomorrow. A vision should show daring, creativity and challenge. It should also be succinct so that it doesn't get lost within itself. Your subject is part of that vision and you should consider how it best fits into the modern direction your school is taking.

Thinking points

● Traditional subject titles, such as maths subject leader or art subject leader, have changed little over the last ten years. However, increasing pressure on timetables, with more and more new subjects, (additional time for PE, high arts appreciation, modern foreign languages and SEAL to name just four new subjects) has forced schools to review how they manage subjects. Increasingly schools are creating amalgamated subject headings, such as arts coordinator to encompass music, DT and art, with these subjects being led by a team. This raises the profile of a collection of subjects and increases the leadership time available by having more people available to lead them.

● Vision equals change and change can be uncomfortable. As a subject leader it is your responsibility to identify what obstacles within your subject(s) may conflict with the school vision so that sensitive and reasonable steps can be taken to embrace everyone.

Tips, ideas and activities

● Certain parts of the vision will be directly relevant to your subject area but remember that you have a corporate responsibility to uphold all of its values.

● You will most likely be expected to write an action plan each year detailing the work you intend to do to develop your subject. When writing an action plan, however, it is a useful exercise to consider what action you might take over a three to five-year period. There is no certainty that you will be in that position for the whole time but having a long-term vision for your subject, based on known need within the school, will support any requests for additional funding if it is paced over a period of time.

● Surveys – particularly online surveys – are a quick way of collecting hard evidence to support opinions but for in-depth knowledge you will need to consider a range of face-to-face opportunities. These may include staff meetings, individual staff consultations, meetings with the school council, parent-school partnership families and other stakeholders such as meal supervisors and teaching assistants. An online survey (such as www.surveymonkey.com) could help you assess subject skills, which will allow you to take appropriate steps for improvement.

● A vision takes time to realise and should then be celebrated (even if it has changed during its journey, which is often inevitable). It is also an appropriate time to evaluate its impact and to determine how, if appropriate, the vision should evolve for the next phase of the school's life.

You Can... **Support the school Self-Evaluation Form (SEF)**

Since 2006 schools have been required to keep an up-to-date school Self-Evaluation Form (SEF). This review document is designed to inform an Ofsted inspection team and direct the school inspection under the new framework for inspection. It is not meant to be a descriptive history of the school but a robust document that is both current and analytical. Although it may be written by the School Leadership Team, there is every chance that you will be required to provide evidence to support statements or to support the writing of key aspects of the SEF.

Thinking points

● The SEF was introduced as a tool to help schools self-evaluate their performance. Its seven sections cross all aspects of school life and provide a snapshot of what is happening in your establishment. Inspectors will use the SEF, national tests data and other available documents to support their judgement of your school.

● The 60-minute lesson observations, that were common with past inspection models, are now history. If you are observed during an inspection it is highly likely that the inspector will only watch you for a few minutes. They are judging that the school has made an accurate evaluation of its teaching within the SEF. You will receive only limited verbal feedback. Inspectors have only one or two days, generally speaking, in which they can gather their evidence, hence the shorter observations.

Tips, ideas and activities

● Although you will not be directly responsible for writing the SEF you may be asked to provide evidence for it. The types of evidence that teachers would be expected to submit include:
  - Action plans (that are part of the School Improvement Plan).
  - End-of-year evaluations of your subject.
  - Copies of lesson observations.
  - Photographs from events.
  - Comments made by parents (such as from key events or during the year).
  - A list of class visits with links to the curriculum.
  - A list of all guest visitors with links to the curriculum.

● If you have not written an or evaluation before, ask to speak to a senior leader who should be able to guide you. Aim to keep your language simple, use short sentences, avoid over-elaboration, identify the key successes and provide an overall evaluation. It should not be long nor should it simply bullet point what happened, as this could lead to misunderstanding.

● The SEF is a joint responsibility and should be communicated to the whole staff body at least once a year. Where there are areas of responsibility, such as the Foundation Stage, the area leader should provide the evidence for that section.

● There are seven sections to the SEF form. These include:
  1. Characteristics of your school.
  2. Views of learners, parents/carers, the community and other stakeholders.
  3. Achievements and standards.
  4. Personal development and well-being.
  5. The quality of provision.
  6. Leadership and management.
  7. Overall effectiveness.

You may be asked to provide evidence for sections 3, 4 and 5.

You Can... Prepare for an HMI inspection

In 2005 a new cycle of schools inspections began, under the then named New Framework for Inspection. It detailed that every three years a school will be inspected (unless deemed unsatisfactory) and that these inspections will be shorter, have a tighter focus and schools will be given shorter notice for inspection (typically 48 hours). Significantly Ofsted now no longer inspects individual subjects in the old-style inspection. This reporting process, although still part of Ofsted, forms a separate inspection.

Thinking points

● Subject inspections are comprised of direct observation of teaching, discussion with staff and pupils, and scrutiny of pupils' work and subject documentation, such as schemes of work. Inspectors evaluate subject achievement, provision, and leadership and management using the same framework and criteria as used in an Ofsted inspection, but interpreted in subject terms.

● Document reference HMI 2489 explains Ofsted's rationale for subject inspections and states that the purpose is to:
  ○ Feed into the Chief Inspector's Annual Report to give a national picture of strengths and areas for development.
  ○ Provide the basis for Ofsted to disseminate findings, including good practice, through its website, conferences, talks and articles.
  ○ Give institutions detailed feedback to help them improve.
  ○ Support institutions' self-evaluation.

Tips, ideas and activities

● Visits to primary schools (including middle schools that are now deemed primary) and any Foundation Stage settings are likely to last only one day, beginning at the start of the school day and ending with feedback towards the end of the teaching day.

● The period of notice for inspections, as with institutional Ofsted inspections, is short. However, as there tends to be a specific focus, which requires a qualified team, the period of notice is likely to be around two weeks rather than 48 hours.

● Your subject may not necessarily be the focus of the inspection but if it is a themed inspection, such as workforce remodelling, you may be required to submit appropriate evidence.

● The cycle for whole-school inspections is currently three years but with survey or subject inspections it is unlikely to be that often. Certainly for primary schools the inspections will be less regular.

● If you have inherited a subject area, you should evaluate the inherited files and paperwork. Anything older than three years should be archived as it is not particularly relevant to the present day. If you have been in post for more than three years, then it is worth 'pruning' your paperwork to ensure it is current, appropriate, has the level of information within it that HMI may be looking for and everything is clearly documented. If, on the other hand, you are leading a new subject area, start as you mean to go on and organise your paperwork carefully!

● Evidence from the inspection should feed back into the school's Self-Evaluation Form (SEF).

You Can... **Manage change**

Schools are in a state of flux. It is a natural process. Certainly schools in the last ten years have been exposed to a great deal of change but change does not mean out with the old and in with the new, as every school has its own idiosyncrasies that make it the place it is. Change is part of school life and when managed carefully, it is a good thing.

Thinking points

● With all aspects of change, particularly institutional change such as a new curriculum, a subject leader should consider its impact on the school and the classroom. Some aspects of change are short-lived. A clear-minded professional should be able to identify these more shallow changes and question their validity. Is it necessary to invest time to understand a new document if it is set to change within a reasonable timeframe? If there is a feeling of doubt, then seek advice from a senior colleague.

● Considered change is good. It creates an evolving learning experience for modern children, and as subject leaders we must be prepared to change. Even if it feels like the wheel has gone full circle, it is not relevant to view the change with a lens from the past as it does not reflect the current community.

Tips, ideas and activities

● As with all aspects of life there are varying levels of change, which require different leadership approaches. Understanding different leadership styles (and particularly knowing your own) will prepare you for different changes within school.

● As a subject leader you will know if there are any significant changes to your subject on the horizon and you should aim to prepare colleagues as soon as possible for these changes. If these are significant you may wish to discuss this with the School Leadership Team first and ask for their advice and support.

● CPD supports any subject change processes. The more you know, the better you will be able to support colleagues.

● One size does not fit all and any change should be adjusted to meet the needs of your school and the children within it.

● Your team (be it phase, year group or subject) is a good place to start when implementing change as your team members are generally your closest allies. Once a significant group of people have adopted any changes that you are implementing, there is often a cascade effect where word of mouth drives the change through the school.

● Review any changes you have introduced and identify strengths and areas for development. These lessons will inform you the next time you are introducing an element of change into the curriculum.

● Michael Fullan is a prolific writer on the subject of change within education and is recognised as a worldwide authority on educational reform. His books include *Change Forces with a Vengeance* (RoutledgeFalmer, 2003) and *Leading in a Culture of Change* (Jossey-Bass, 2001). He has also written many articles. To find out more information, visit www.michaelfullan.ca

You Can... Deal with conflict

Conflict and change are part of a teacher's life. Given the broad social spectrum of situations teachers are exposed to, it is inevitable that at some point in their careers teachers will be involved in conflict. It is how we deal with it that's half the battle and how we manage it to help to create a positive outcome. However, if dealt with inappropriately the result can be destructive and rarely in the best interests of both parties.

Thinking points

Conflict is often an indicator of other pressures outside of the school falling into the classroom. Rarely is it meant to be personal, although at the time this might not seem the case. It is important that, in times of conflict, teachers keep a professional distance and dialogue with the involved parties. This is not to dehumanise conversations but care must be taken not to exacerbate the conflict. It is likely that carers may want to apologise once they have considered the school's point of view and it is important that you are able to steer the conversation so that is possible. It is good for the school, the carer's relationship with you and ultimately the child.

Tips, ideas and activities

● Parents and school staff must work closely together in order to quickly resolve any problems. Having an open-door climate demonstrates that a school is willing to listen and is robust enough to address any complaints. Complaints may well be justified and ultimately lessons can be learned to improve practice.

● Keep to the specifics of the conflict and be willing to offer creative alternatives. Keeping the focus tight will support everybody's understanding of the outcomes.

● When working with children, we challenge their behaviour and not their personality. Similarly, deal with the issues of a complaint or conflict and not the emotions or personalities.

● There are few times when compromise cannot be achieved. Consider where you are willing to place yourself when compromising. If you feel that your position is resolute, you may wish to consider involving a mediator or seeking advice from a senior leader – they can at least act as a sounding board. However, be reasonable and ensure that your expectations are realistic.

● If necessary, set goals. Long-term goals supported by short-term goals will help guide the conflict in managed steps.

● Once a resolution has been agreed, both parties need to commit to it. It is reasonable to review this position at regular intervals until the commitment is well established.

● Ultimately we rely upon one another to ensure the smooth operation of a dynamic institute. Confidence must be fostered by all parties and it is therefore essential to build relationships, however sensitive the issue, in the best interests of the child.

You Can... **Recognise your contribution**

A headteacher once said of his talented staff that they all had an incurable illness that, in many ways, made them so good. The illness was self-criticism. It is something that, as a profession, we are very good at. However, recognising your contribution towards a child's learning is equally valuable. This supports your assessment of their progress and, in what is a very busy job, gives you a measure of your impact.

Thinking points

● Teachers' contributions should never be underestimated. An inspiring teacher can shape and change pupils' aspirations in a way that affects their whole lives (it is why I became a writer).

● Although we are not particularly good at celebrating teachers' contributions, it is something that we should be proud of. For the last 25 years, China has held a National Day for Teachers to celebrate and uphold the good work performed by the nation's millions of teachers. Indeed there are national teachers' days in 28 countries around the world including America, Australia, Russia and China.

● In the UK we have the annual Teachers' Awards (nicknamed the Teachers' Oscars). If you have a colleague who you feel is worthy of praise, talk to your line manager and nominate them – even if they do not receive an award they will appreciate the credit you have given them.

Tips, ideas and activities

● How closely do you evaluate your action plan? We have busy lives and it can be challenging enough to just 'tick' the 'action done' box and move on to the next demanding piece of work. But that does not allow for any evaluation, particularly if something has gone well. Questions should be raised to unpick why the piece of work was so successful in order to replicate it or share it with other establishments.

● Taking time with a colleague during a PPA period to review the successes of the term or half-term is satisfying and can be an incentive to get to the end of term.

● There are an increasing number of courses that, as part of them, perform what are referred to as 360-degree reviews of your contribution to school life by interviewing a group of colleagues. It can be a challenging process but almost always produces concrete evidence that either supports your current good practice or clearly indicates how you could improve it.

● Celebration is good for the soul! Aim to keep part of a budget for 'staffroom treats' after a high-profile event (such as a curriculum day or week) to thank colleagues for their hard work in making it a success.

● Performance management is a focused tool that can act as a place to discuss achievement over the last academic year. Within this forum, achievements beyond the targets set can be considered and it is an ideal opportunity for formal praise.

● Encouraging colleagues and celebrating aspects of their work, either verbally, by email or in a short note, really lifts the spirits and is an endorsement that you think they are doing things right.

You Can... **Use books to support your leadership**

It was only in 2003 that the National College for School Leadership (NCSL) first produced research papers on middle leadership and equally publishers have taken time to print books on this subject. However, there are a growing number of useful books that can help point you in the right direction or provide useful advice. Also, there are plenty of books in bookshops on leadership within the business world and many of these have lessons that can be transferred to leadership in schools.

Thinking points

● As a leader it is in your best interests to be current in your thinking. Briefing events will help but you will have a large of amount of reading to consume. Read with care and intelligence. Do not be afraid to skim but equally do not skim to the point where you have taken nothing in. It is a skill but one that can be refined with time.

● Publications from the Department for Children, Schools and Families (DCSF) need to be requested from the department's publications team as they are rarely sent directly to schools. Alternatively consider downloading publications from the DCSF website: www.dcsf.gov.uk.

Tips, ideas and activities

● A fun and easy-to-read book is the *Leadership Pocketbook* by Fiona Elsa Dent (part of the *Pocketbook* range by Management Pocketbooks). It is a tiny book with one nugget of information per page. Subjects covered include 'the nature of leadership', 'leaders and teams', 'key skills', and 'leading change'.

● In the same vein is *Leadership for Dummies* by Marshall Loeb & Stephen Kindel (Wiley & Sons, 1999). The dummies range is famous for its straightforward, fun way of approaching subjects, and leadership follows this model. Alongside this book are *Managing Teams for Dummies* (John Wiley and Sons, 2002) and *Communicating Effectively for Dummies* (John Wiley and Sons, 2001) both by Marty Brounstein.

● *How to Lead* by Jo Owen (Pearson Education, 2005) covers most modern aspects of leadership. It is an insightful and witty book that opens with the dilemma of many modern leaders: what most people value as a leader is the ability to motivate others, the modern dilemma is that all too often there isn't anybody to motivate (which may be particularly true as a middle leader).

● Malcolm Gladwell is author of *The Tipping Point* and *Blink* (Little Brown Book Group, 2002 and 2006) both of which are explorations of how we think, what affects our decisions and how to capitalise on those decisions. His style is sharp and intelligent – a good summer read!

You Can... **Use the internet to support your leadership**

When the current National Curriculum was developed, just over ten years ago, we had no idea what impact the internet would have on all aspects of our lives. Today we use it for ordering our food, checking our bank balance, research and social networking. It is a powerful tool and, thanks to the investment into broadband technology, it is something that is available for all teachers to use at a speed that meets their expectation. It is central to the communications revolution and it is a powerful and fast resource.

Thinking points

● Internet-based training is taking off as a form of open-access training that is available when you need it. This has its uses in that it can fit around busy lives, however, it should be viewed with caution. In the same way that computers will never replace teachers in the classroom, internet-based training should never replace face-to-face training.

● Know where to access relevant information. Governors' briefing notes will indicate short-term actions and the DCSF's website (www.standards.dcsf.gov.uk) will contain all common documents. If a document is only available as a PDF (Portable Document Format), as is increasingly the case, you must be able to access and store it. If you do not know how to do this, it is important to find out.

Tips, ideas and activities

● The National College for School Leadership (NCSL) is the country's foremost provider of high-quality leadership material. The courses they run (see page 16 about professional development) contain internet-based modules that are complimented by face-to-face training days. For more information, visit www.ncsl.org.uk.

● Learn how to add attachments to your emails. Each system has a slightly different way of doing it but this will allow you to share documents quickly with colleagues.

● There are an increasing number of websites that will allow you to create online surveys (www.surveymonkey.com is a good example). A survey can be created fairly quickly, with links emailed to colleagues, classes or the whole school. The advantage of these systems is that they generate the data as soon as somebody has completed the survey, making it fast and accurate.

● Increasingly schools are changing how they communicate with families. Over the last few years most schools have developed their own websites and now more schools are adding to their digital communication by emailing and texting parents appropriately. This is a relatively inexpensive form of communication which can ensure that a copy of a letter sent home in the book bag has also been emailed to a carer.

● Podcasts from the BBC can help you keep up to date with current events.

● If you do not have the time to read a book it is likely you will be able to obtain an audio version of it to listen to. Although not as effective as reading it will allow you to listen to it while in the car, on a train or bus. Websites such as www.audible.com have a comprehensive list of titles.

You Can... **Ensure every child matters**

The Government presented Every Child Matters (ECM) *in 2003 as a new approach to the well-being of all children regardless of background or circumstance. All agencies that work with children, including health, social services and education, are being moulded to support children as best as possible. All of this is to avoid the tragic circumstances of Victoria Climbié, the girl who sparked this change across all services, happening again.*

Thinking points

● There are five key *Every Child Matters* outcomes. These are:
- Be healthy
- Stay safe
- Enjoy and achieve
- Make a positive contribution
- Achieve economic well-being.

● The *ECM* agenda is enormous. No one school leader and no one school can manage it alone. Effective school leaders will need to harness their colleagues' strengths and, through creative use of TLR points, re-structure their school leadership so that it can begin to address the *ECM* outcomes with true meaning.

● The *ECM* website (www. everychildmatters.gov.uk) provides plenty of food for thought.

Tips, ideas and activities

● Being healthy can be reflected in your own practice. Eating a healthy snack at break times will act as a model for children and encourage them to choose a healthy option. Equally consider how you travel to school. If you live close enough then walk or cycle – children love seeing a cycle champion, particularly if it is their teacher.

● Staying safe forms a seasonal aspect of school life, as well as the day to day safeguarding of individuals. Autumn is a good opportunity to remind children of stranger danger if they go out on Halloween and fire protection for Guy Fawkes Night. Winter is a time for reminding children to wear warm, reflective clothing so that they are seen in the dark. Spring and summer are good times to review road safety when children are out and about more often.

● School should be full of enjoyment. Celebrate the fun and achievement in your classroom. Ask your children how they want their class set out and involve them in this process to give them ownership of a space they occupy for as much of the year as you do!

● You can be proactive in supporting children to make a positive contribution to the community. This could be guiding children to run a stall at the winter or summer school fair, taking a choir out to another school or local home, or supporting older children to work with younger ones as a designated buddy.

● Supporting economic well-being is, of all the *ECM* objectives, least tangible for primary schools. That said, money is part of the maths curriculum. Your school may run a tuck shop and it is highly likely that there will be fundraising events going on at school. Take time to identify the importance of these events so that children can recognise the positive impact the event is having.

You Can... **Have an awareness of the Primary Review**

The Primary Review is a wide-ranging and independent enquiry into the state and future of primary education in England. It is perhaps the most comprehensive investigation since the publication of the Plowden Report in 1967. The Review is focusing on ten themes that are central to the processes and procedures of primary schools in England: purposes and value, learning and teaching, curriculum and assessment, quality and standards, diversity and inclusion, settings and professionals, parenting, caring and educating, beyond the school, structures and phases, and funding and governance.

Thinking points
● Bringing families and the community into the debate is seen as central to the Primary Review. It is another reflection of the growing change that schools face. No longer are they isolated institutes (and many would argue they have never been) but now schools need to address how they can get into the community and how the community can get into them.

● Running alongside the Primary Review, but not related, is the Primary Curriculum Review led by Sir Jim Rose, former director of Ofsted. This review is focusing on what is being taught in our schools and although there are clear indications of what it will contain (subject specialists and some subjects likely to amalgamate) this is not an independent report, as the Primary Review is, and will be reflecting current government aims. It is, arguably, an interim review that will give class teachers greater freedom when planning their teaching.

Tips, ideas and activities
● The Review soundings are conveniently written in two forms: full documents and summaries. The summaries are rarely more than two pages long and highlight key points.

● The impact of the Review will be long-lasting. To date it has only released eight press statements yet five of these have formed major news. There is little doubt that the full Review (to be published in summer 2009) will stir political and social discussions. The full document is likely to run to many pages but a summary document will be provided so that you are able to digest the key points.

● With your phase or year partner, share sections of the Review to digest. Sharing what you have read will not only reinforce those aspects for you but it is also a good use of time.

● You will naturally be drawn to aspects of the report that either reflect the school's good practice or that you feel are relevant to school development.

● One of the core purposes of the Review is to review the learning environment. This is an opportunity for you to consider the learning environment you are exposing children to on a daily basis. There will be certain things that are out of your control (such as a total redecoration) but how you set out displays, label your room, organise the furniture will impact on children's learning on a daily basis. Visiting colleagues' rooms will give you ideas (this can be done after school or during PPA time) or take time to visit another school.

● It is a policy document for the future but the planning for it must be addressed today.

● The Primary Review publications can be found at www.primaryreview.org.uk

You Can... **Plan your career**

At heart only you know how you want your career to evolve and that will be a balance between your own personal circumstances and career aspirations. Equally, planning a career does not always mean planning to be upwardly mobile. There are many opportunities that teachers can take to broaden their experiences that are not directly linked to vertical promotion. In the end, this is our only shot at life and one that should be done wisely with a balance of challenge and enjoyment.

Thinking points

● Life coaches have been commonplace in business for several years and are increasingly filtering into schools. We are a generation who, for the first time, can choose to dip in and out of various careers and use these experiences to enhance our working lives. A life coach can help to plan a career or a new direction.

● There is a wide choice of overseas opportunities for British-trained teachers. A range of schemes from teacher swap in America or Japan to working in any number of international schools across the world are available. The DCSF Teacher's International Development programme provides teachers with short-term visit opportunities to experience best practice international schools. It is supported by over 50 countries with an annual investment of £3 million. For more information visit www.teachernet.gov.uk and search for 'Teacher's International Development Programme'.

Tips, ideas and activities

● Research is an increasingly important aspect of the profession and can be funded through a variety of charitable grants and bursaries.

- The British Ecological Society offers a range of awards for ecologically based research. Visit www.britishecologicalsociety.org and search for 'grants and prizes'.
- The Centre for British Teachers (www.cfbt.com) has over 40 years of experience supporting research in education and clear systems for accessing funding.
- The large teaching unions also offer awards for research (NASUWT, NUT and NAHT). For further information approach a local union representative.

● Career breaks can prove to be a valuable time to recharge and try something new. There are a variety of options but, essentially, if you are considering taking a career break, then it is best to discuss the length of time away from class as soon as possible with your line manager. Many charities such as Outreach International and VSO are looking for mature professionals to work as volunteers. Alternatively, it may be a time to write that book you have always wanted to. Whatever your intentions, a career break can offer a rare period of time away from the profession.

● Secondments into other sectors of education or industry can live up to the saying 'a change is as good as a rest'. They offer stimulation and a valuable opportunity to view your practice from a different angle. They do not necessarily need to be blocked periods of time (however, even a micro-secondment of a week can be valuable) but can be a day or two a week out of class. Heads, Teachers and Industry (www.hti.org.uk) is a charity that can arrange a variety of placements in industry and business for heads and teachers.

You Can... Assess risk

Risk assessment and safety are key areas of responsibility of the school. It is the headteacher's duty to ensure that appropriate personnel are placed to cover and monitor all potential areas of risk. Where risk is identified, the headteacher must take appropriate action to manage the risk and reduce its potential impact. Equally, it is every staff member's duty to act on areas of potential risk by having the skills to identify where these risks might occur and who to approach.

Thinking points

● In health and safety terms a 'hazard' is any situation that could cause harm, such as a slippery floor, or an unsafe act like 'horseplay' or locations around the site that are of potential danger, such as unofficial 'short cuts'. Within this 'risk' is the potential it poses to an individual. It is, therefore, the establishment's responsibility to identify that risk and manage it.

● Children with particular needs, such as those in wheelchairs, will present new potential hazards that require risk assessments. Your local authority should be able to provide advice and support as well as the parents or previous school (if applicable).

● A failure to manage risk can not only have human and financial impacts but can also damage the reputation of the school. A good reputation is important when attracting families and staff as it reflects good management.

Tips, ideas and activities

● Do you know who is on the health and safety committee? The committee members should include the child protection officer, educational visits coordinator, a fire marshal, health officer (usually your primary first aider), site manager and the headteacher, who has overall responsibility.

● Do you follow all educational visit risk procedures? It could be argued that it is a child's right to be taken on educational visits but equally it is the teacher's responsibility to ensure that any appropriate risk assessment forms and adult checks have been completed in good time before the visit.

● Each class must have a clear set of fire evacuation procedures. These should be practised at least half a term with the fire marshal noting the time of day and length of time taken for the practice. For the first practice of the year, ensure the class know what to do, particularly if they are young. This will make them feel secure and help the drill run smoothly. If you are teaching very young children and are aware that a drill has been planned at a particularly vulnerable time in the day, such as PE when they will be dressed in light clothes rather than day clothes, raise this with a line manager who may be in a position to adjust the time.

● Most risk occurs when off-site. When planning a trip, attempt to visit the site well before the children are scheduled to visit. This will give you plenty of time to assess any potential risks and plan for them accordingly.

● It is not possible to be able to plan for every eventuality. If an extraordinary event occurs (such as sudden flooding) you must evaluate the risk there and then and act promptly to minimise its impact.

You Can... **Ensure that there are appropriate checks**

As a subject leader you will want to encourage classes to go on educational visits or have specialists in to talk to the class. In the current climate you will be aware of the sensitivity of involving parents and other adults in this process. As schools we want to encourage carers into the classroom to share in their child's learning but proper safeguarding must be taken to ensure that this is not at the risk of the other children or yourself.

Thinking points

● The response to the murders of Jessica Chapman and Holly Wells in Soham in 2001 was the Bichard enquiry, led by Sir Michael Bichard. The resulting safeguarding measures have brought a renewed emphasis on criminal checks for all adults working with or around young people and children. It is part of the darker side of education but necessary as a commitment to preventing such a tragedy happening again.

● Full child protection training is expensive and not necessary for all members of staff but it is important to have a basic understanding of major issues:
  ● The four types of abuse (see page 54)
  ● What child protection is (see page 53)
  ● How to safely be part of a recruitment process (see page 55).

Tips, ideas and activities

● All educational visits should have a sensible risk assessment. In principle, this means identifying what risks might be associated with going off-site. These could include necessary road crossings, aspects of the site you are visiting and how many children you are taking with you. Ratios of staff to children are an important factor. In general the DCSF *Health and Safety of Pupils on Educational Visits* guidelines give the following ratios:
  ● One adult for every 10–15 pupils in school years 4 to 6.
  ● One adult for every six pupils in school years 1 to 3 (under 5s reception classes should have a higher ratio of adults to pupils).
  ● An informal recommendation of one adult to every two children is given for nursery.

● Who you take is of great importance. Not only is it not always possible to use exclusively school staff, it is not always desirable. School visits are a useful way for parents to involve themselves in school life. How schools check other adults has changed a great deal in recent years and it is important to find out what the current procedures are with your school travel coordinator.

● A List 99 check is a low-impact search conducted on your behalf by your local authority (though there is a nominal charge for each check) to identify any criminal records. To conduct a check you will need the person's full name, any previous names (such as maiden names or names prior to Deed Poll changes), their date of birth and current address. This is only required if an adult is alone with the children, such as with a group.

● A CRB check does not need to be undertaken for occasional visits. This is a thorough check of an individual's history and can take up to three months to complete. It is also quite expensive.

You Can... **Begin to understand child protection**

A child protection officer has an almost unique position within a school; they act as a central point of reference for a wide range of services. Lord Laming's report, Keeping Children Safe, following the death of Victoria Climbié, identified the need for different agencies to work together to ensure good practice across all groups and to learn lessons from this tragic event. It is an important part of the role of the child protection officer to ensure that communication is concise, timely and relevant.

Thinking points

● Each school should have a senior member of the School Leadership Team who is designated to take lead responsibility for dealing with child protection issues. They should provide advice and support to other staff, liaise with the local authority, and work with other agencies. They should be somebody who has access to all agencies and generally tends to be the headteacher as they also bring their own authority.

● Teachers tend to be at the front line of child protection. Being able to identify a child who is at risk – be it from emotional, physical, sexual abuse or neglect – is the sharp end of education. Not knowing what to look for is not an excuse. If you have not had any recent child protection training you should be able to at least read the child protection guidance on your local authority's website. Knowing what to look out for could save precious time.

Tips, ideas and activities

● Have you had recent child protection training? If you have gone more than two years without any significant child protection training then you should inform the professional development coordinator as a matter of urgency.

● Check who your child protection officer is. It is most likely to be your headteacher or SENCO but they will be the designated person responsible for 'looked-after children' and those who are on the register of children who are at risk in any form. It is your duty to inform them of any concerns that you have as quickly as possible.

● If you have been put in the position where you have had to restrain a child, because they pose a risk of harm to themselves or others, ensure that after the incident you record how you acted and why. A form for this purpose is provided on page 62. This should then be submitted to the headteacher or senior leader who is managing the situation. Although laws are changing, it must be transparent why you acted in the manner that you did.

● If a child has disclosed anything to you, record what has been said exactly. Do not elaborate and refrain from asking leading questions. If you have sufficient cause for concern, speak to the child protection officer or your line manager.

● Ultimately the over-arching principle of all child protection is the welfare of the child and therefore no information can be kept in confidence if there is any risk to the child. A teacher has a duty of care to all children and therefore you should not make promises of trust to a child when it is against their well-being and compromises safeguarding policies.

● A full copy of Lord Laming's report, Keeping Children Safe, can be obtained from http://publications.teachernet.gov.uk by searching for 'Keeping Children Safe Victoria Climbié'.

You Can... **Be aware of abuse**

Identifying a child who you believe to be in an abusive situation at home is what all teachers fear, not for themselves but for the child and family involved. It is, fortunately, rare (rarer than the papers would let us believe) but nonetheless some children are living in fear in one form or another on a daily basis. Being able to identify what form of abuse is taking place is the first step to prevention and supporting the child and their family.

Thinking points

● There are four categories of abuse as defined in paragraph 6.40 of the document *Working Together Under the Children Act* (1989):
  ● **Neglect:** persistent or severe neglect, or the failure to protect a child from exposure to any kind of danger, including cold or starvation, or extreme failure to carry out important aspects of care, resulting in the significant impairment of the child's health or development, including non-organic failure to thrive;
  ● **Physical injury:** actual or likely physical injury to a child, or failure to prevent physical injury (or suffering) to a child including deliberate poisoning, suffocation and Munchausen's syndrome by proxy;
  ● **Sexual abuse:** actual or likely sexual exploitation of a child or adolescent. The child may be dependent and/or developmentally immature;
  ● **Emotional abuse:** actual or likely severe adverse effect on the emotional and behavioural development of a child caused by persistent or severe emotional ill-treatment or rejection.

Tips, ideas and activities

● How abuse is reported is extremely important. Inconsistencies in reports could lead to the wrong action being taken or, perhaps worse, no action at all. Your school should have a common incident report sheet (usually a photocopy) that everybody knows how to complete. If you are not sure, then speak to your SENCO, child protection officer or headteacher. When writing a report keep it factual, and avoid unnecessary description and emotive language (for example, 'she screamed madly at me' could be re-written as 'she shouted at me'. Words such as 'shouted' will often speak for themselves).

● If a child has made a disclosure to you, be careful how you pursue any enquiry. Your role is to inform the child protection officer as soon as possible and to correctly record any disclosure, not to conduct an investigation.

● Your local authority will have their own definitions of the four forms of abuse and knowing them will support the school in reporting abuse.

● Of all the areas of abuse, emotional abuse is arguably the hardest to define. Knowing how your local authority defines it can be useful. What is important is to record your concerns and to share them with the nominated child protection officer (often the headteacher) as soon as possible.

● A family support worker can be used by schools for early intervention before involving the full force of social services. Most schools will have access to one via their local children's centre or network of local schools (often referred to as a Local Area Network). Your SENCO should be able to support you.

You Can... **Support a recruitment committee**

Recruitment has a natural cycle, with the majority of teaching staff recruitment falling between March and May. Recruitment carries a high risk as successful candidates, if successful, will go on to join you in representing your school. You will want to know that the candidate is not only right for the school but will ensure the ongoing safeguarding of pupils. Although you may not be directly involved in all aspects of recruitment it is good practice to involve middle managers if there is a clear line of responsibility with the new position.

Thinking points

● Safeguarding procedures should be set within your school's recruitment procedures to ensure that the person recruited will reflect the safe environment of your school. That said, the Bichard Inquiry Report stated that 'the harsh reality is that if a sufficiently devious person is determined to seek out opportunities to work their evil, no one can guarantee they will be stopped. Our task is to make it as difficult as possible for them to succeed...' We must be vigilant.

● Your job description should include a reference that either the school or local authority have adopted safer recruitment procedures. It is their duty to highlight the well-being of children in their care and it subsequently becomes your duty once you have agreed your contract. It is something that most teachers have informally understood for years.

Tips, ideas and activities

● You may be asked to be part of an interview panel. This will be because you bring a set of skills and may be a line manager or direct colleague. Clarify this if you are not sure why you have been asked.

● Have you received any recruitment training? Do you understand the role you are going to take? Has the job specification and description been clearly defined?

● Are you clear about the type of interview to be conducted? A teacher may be required to teach, so classes will need to be arranged. When you are observing a teacher teaching, ask for a common set of guidelines for the observation. The Ofsted guidelines for classroom observations can be used if none are available at school. It is likely that the whole panel will observe the lesson. The process of agreeing the grade is a useful process and is a rare opportunity for evaluating teaching.

● The standard procedure for recruitment is:
1. Advertise the post including personal specifications.
2. Send out information packs.
3. Shortlist candidates for interview (this should be done by a minimum of two people and not alone).
4. Obtain references (unless the candidate has requested they be obtained after the interview). General references should not be accepted alone. Even if the applicant has come from overseas, with modern technology it is relatively straightforward to obtain a current reference.
5. Invite candidates to the interview.
6. Conduct interview and then 'score' the candidates.
7. Make a conditional offer of employment pending all checks.

● The document *Safeguarding Children and Safer Recruitment in Education* can be downloaded from http://publications teachernet.gov.uk.

To do

Subject area: _____

Name: _____ Date: _____

This week

Talk to:

-
-
-
-
-

Budget:

-
-
-
-
-

Action from improvement plan:

-
-
-
-
-

This half-term

Talk to:

-
-
-
-
-

Budget:

-
-
-
-
-

Action from improvement plan:

-
-
-
-
-

Subject leader calendar – autumn term

When	What	Who	Notes on action
September	Performance management objective setting.	Teachers, teaching assistants, performance management team leaders.	
September	Initial subject leadership team meetings.	All coordinators.	
October	Discuss local authority data analysis for literacy and numeracy (KS1 and KS2) and Foundation Stage profiles. Look at implications for school improvement.	Senior Leadership Team (SLT), Foundation Stage coordinator.	
October	First parent consultations.	Class teachers.	
October	Assessment week: review of children's progress levelling for reading, writing, maths.	Class teachers.	
November	Monitor planning in all year groups.	All coordinators.	
November	Set Y2 and Y6 targets for current Y1 and Y5.	Y1 and Y5 class teachers in conjunction with SLT.	
November	Pupil-tracking sheets updated. Groups identified for intervention. Data collected and analysed.	Class teachers. Coordinators and SLT.	
November	Pupil conferencing and target sharing.	Class teachers, pupils.	
November	Team leader and mentor leadership meeting: focus – action planning.	Subject coordinators, SLT.	
December	Staff questionnaire to evaluate staff views on literacy and numeracy; Continuing Professional Development; ethos and support; other aspects of school functioning. SLT analysis to consider implications arising from staff questionnaire.	All staff, SLT.	

Subject leader calendar – spring term

When	What	Who	Notes on action
January	Update Continuing Professional Development programme in line with identified school improvement priorities.	Subject leaders, School Leadership Team (SLT).	
February	Subject scrutiny (typically a book scrutiny or similar task).	Subject coordinators, SLT.	
February	Mid-year subject leadership team meetings to review progress.	Subject coordinators.	
February	Assessment week: review of children's progress. Pupil questionnaire conducted during assessment week and analysed.	Class teachers. SLT.	
Feb/March	Second parent consultations.	All teachers.	
March	Interim performance management reviews.	Headteacher, deputy headteacher, performance management team leaders, teachers and support staff.	
March	Performance management lesson observations.	Headteacher, deputy headteacher, performance management team leaders.	
March	Identify budget needs for the coming year based on school improvement priorities, last year's budget and known needs, and place requests to headteacher.	Subject coordinator.	
March	Review budget and draft profile.	Admin staff, headteacher, governing body.	
March	Pupil-tracking sheets updated and analysed. Interventions evaluated. Data collected and reviewed.	All staff and SLT. Literacy and numeracy coordinators.	
March	Pupil conferencing and target sharing.	Teachers and pupils.	
March	Team leader and mentor leadership meeting: focus – budget setting.	Subject coordinators, SLT.	
March	Focus week to evaluate standards in foundation subjects.	Foundation subject coordinators, SLT.	

Subject leader calendar – summer term

When	What	Who	Notes on action
April/May	Adjust Continuing Professional Development programme in line with identified school improvement priorities.	School Leadership Team (SLT).	
May/June	Assessment fortnight: review of children's progress.	All teaching staff.	
June	Pupil-tracking sheets updated and analysed. Science and ICT National Curriculum levels recorded. Data collected by SLT and relevant coordinators.	All teaching staff, coordinators, SLT.	
June	Pupil conferencing and target sharing.	All teaching staff.	
June	Subject leadership team meetings: review action plan from previous year and identify action/needs for the coming year.	Subject coordinators.	
June	Review progress in achieving school improvement priorities for current academic year. Identify priorities emerging for coming year.	All teaching staff, governing body.	
June	Focus week to evaluate standards in foundation subjects.	Foundation subject coordinators.	
July	Performance management review meetings.	Teachers, teaching assistants, performance management team leaders.	
July	Parent/carer questionnaire.	Parent governors, SLT.	
July	Team leader and mentor leadership meeting: focus – writing an action plan and reviewing the previous action plan as a document to governors	Subject coordinators, SLT.	
July	Coordinators' action plans reviewed and written in line with School Improvement Plan (SIP).	Curriculum coordinators..	
July	Third parent consultation evenings and end-of-year review of pupil progress.	Teachers and parents.	
July	Plan CPD programme in line with identified school improvement priorities: coordinators to identify training needs for the coming year.	Subject coordinators, SLT.	
July	Review of INSET and new draft plan drawn up for next academic year, training days set.	SLT.	

Communication with other adults

Name of adult: _____   Name of teacher: _____

Date: _____   Time of lesson: _____

Class: _____   Curriculum area: _____

Lesson objective: _____

Children in focus group:

Key questions:

Lesson brief:

Notes on children's progress:

Assessment:

Additional comments:

Subject improvement plan

School name:	Links to school aims/vision:	*ECM* outcomes: ● Being healthy ● Staying safe ● Enjoying and achieving ● Making a positive contribution ● Economic well-being
Subject leader:	Objectives:	
Academic year:		Success outcomes:

Actions required (steps to be taken)	Action by whom	Action by when	Funding	Monitoring – how and who	Notes on progress

Incident report

Name of child(ren): _____ Class: _____ Date: _____

Where did the incident take place?

What did the child do and/or what was said? (include what appeared to trigger the behaviour)

Who was involved and/or who saw the incident?

What action has already been taken?

How will this be followed up and by whom?	Date action completed

Signed: _____

Date: _____

Copy to be given to headteacher.

Index

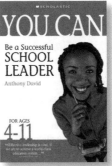

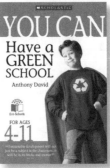

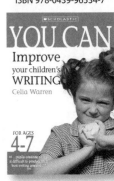
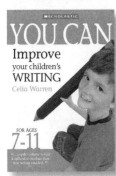